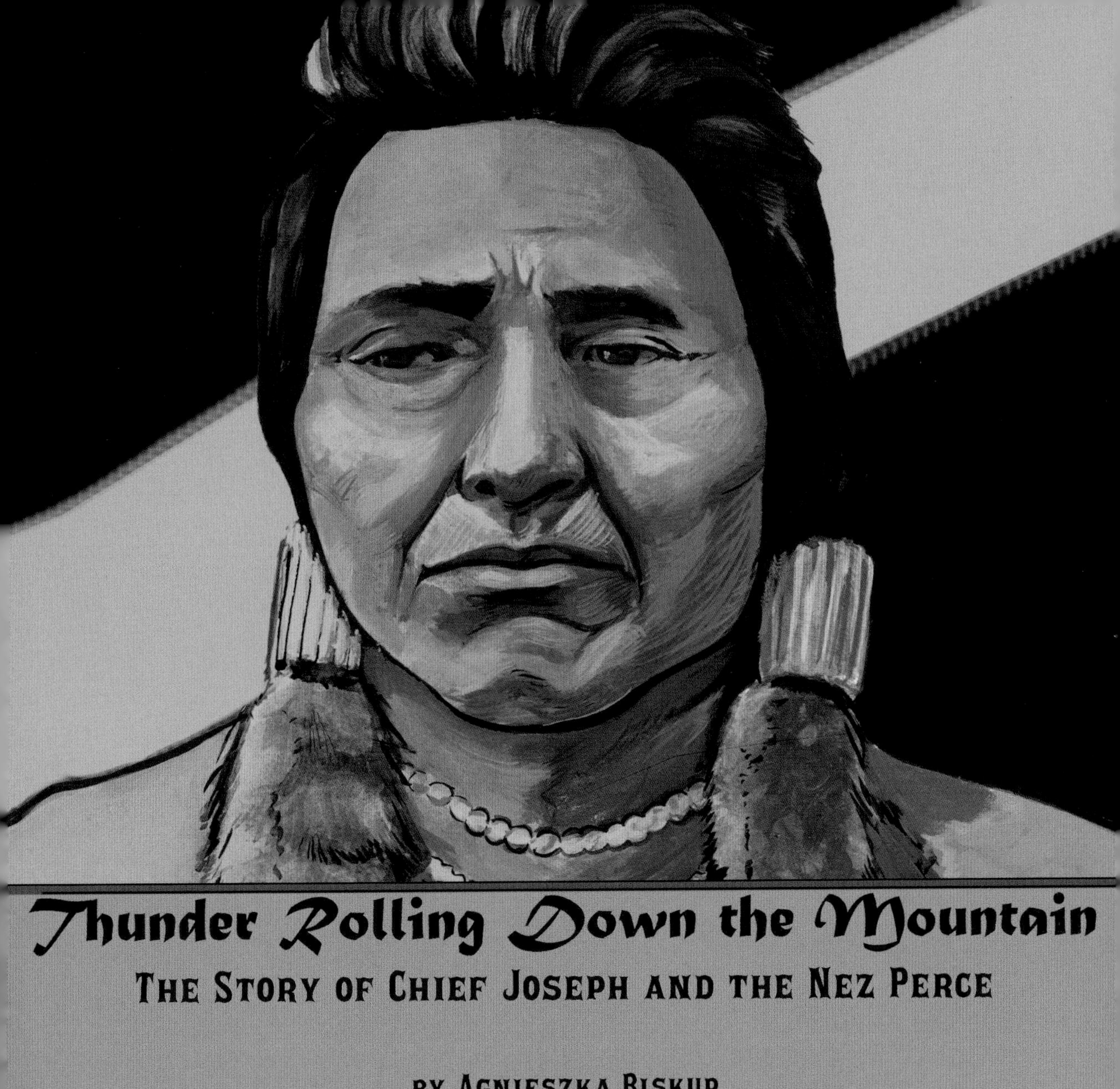

Thunder Rolling Down the Mountain

The Story of Chief Joseph and the Nez Perce

by Agnieszka Biskup

illustrated by Rusty Zimmerman

Consultant:
Dr. Troy Johnson
Chair, American Indian Studies Program
California State University, Long Beach

CAPSTONE PRESS
a capstone imprint

Graphic Library is published by Capstone Press,

151 Good Counsel Drive, P.O. Box 669, Mankato, Minnesota 56002.

www.capstonepub.com

Books published by Capstone Press are manufactured with paper containing at least 10 percent post-consumer waste.

Library of Congress Cataloging-in-Publication Data

Biskup, Agnieszka.
Thunder rolling down the mountain : the story of Chief Joseph and the Nez Perce / Agnieszka Biskup ; illustrated by Rusty Zimmerman.
p. cm.—(Graphic library. American graphic)
Includes bibliographical references and index.
  Summary: "In graphic novel format, explores the battles and hardships faced by Chief Joseph and the Nez Perce when they were forced to leave their homelands"—Provided by publisher.
ISBN 978-1-4296-5472-2 (library binding)
ISBN 978-1-4296-6270-3 (paperback)
1. Joseph, Nez Percé Chief, 1840–1904—Comic books, strips, etc.—Juvenile literature. 2. Nez Percé Indians—Kings and rulers—Biography—Comic books, strips, etc.—Juvenile literature. 3. Nez Percé Indians—Wars, 1877—Comic books, strips, etc.—Juvenile literature. 4. Nez Percé Indians—History—19th century—Comic books, strips, etc.—Juvenile literature. 5. Graphic novels. I. Zimmerman, Rusty, ill. II. Title. III. Series.
E99.N5J5823 2011
979.5004'974124—dc22
[B]
                          2010027914

Direct quotations appear in yellow bubbles on the following pages:

Page 8 and page 9 (bottom), from "An Indian's Views of Indian Affairs by Young Joseph, Chief of the Nez Perce" (The North American Review, vol. 0128, issue 269, April 1879) <http://digital.library.cornell.edu>

Page 9 (top), from The Flight of the Nez Perce by Mark H. Brown (Lincoln, Neb.: University of Nebraska Press, 1967)

Pages 26–27, from Chief Joseph: Guardian of the People by Candy Moulton (New York: Forge Books, 2005)

Photo Credits:
Courtesy of Pendleton Woolen Mills Archives, 28; Shutterstock/akva, 29; US Forest Service, Nez Perce National Historic Trail, 20-21

Art Director: Nathan Gassman

Editor: Lori Shores

Media Researcher: Wanda Winch

Production Specialist: Eric Manske

Printed in the United States of America in Stevens Point, Wisconsin.
092010   005934WZS11

TABLE of CONTENTS

CHAPTER 1 FLIGHT

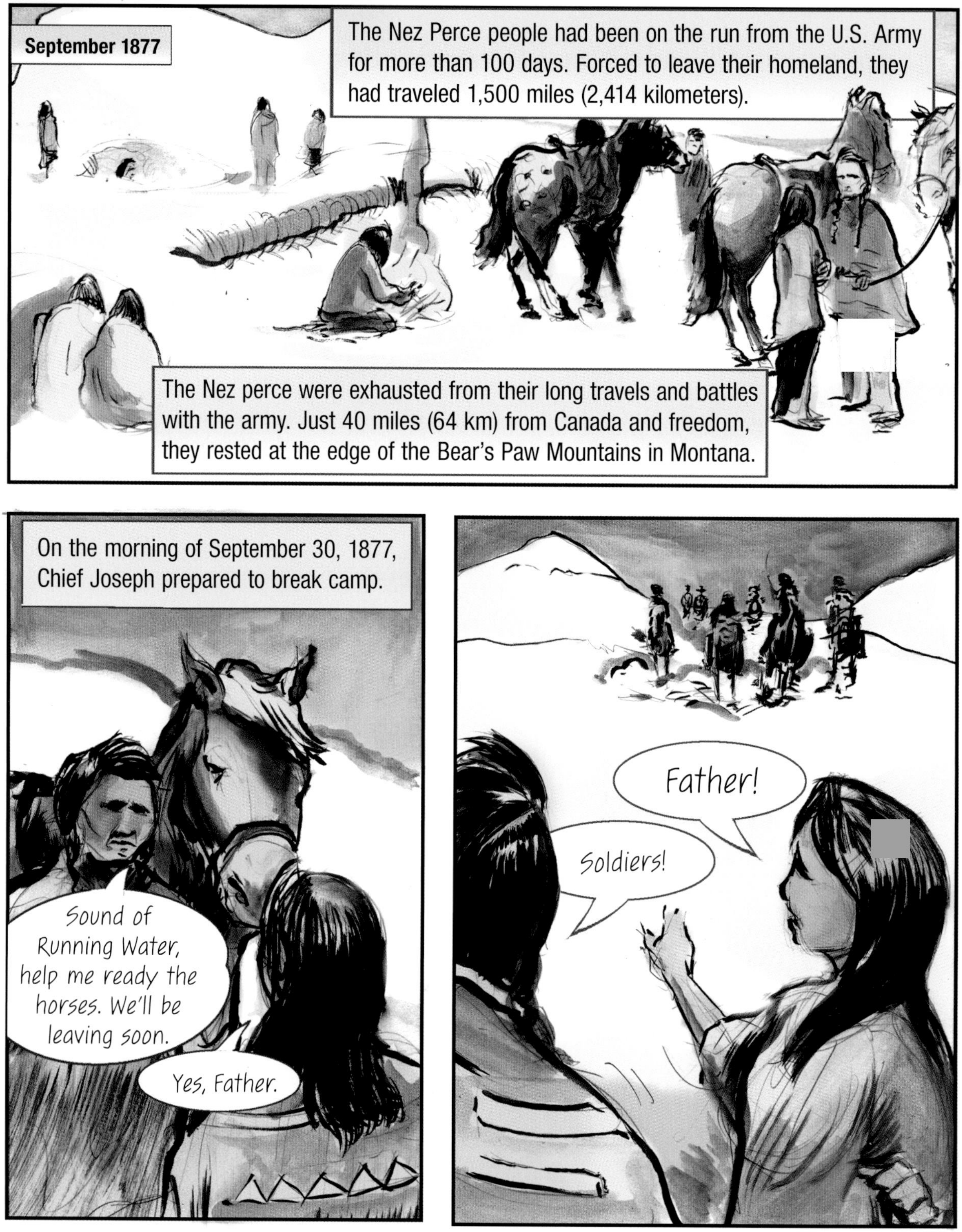
September 1877
The Nez Perce people had been on the run from the U.S. Army for more than 100 days. Forced to leave their homeland, they had traveled 1,500 miles (2,414 kilometers).
The Nez perce were exhausted from their long travels and battles with the army. Just 40 miles (64 km) from Canada and freedom, they rested at the edge of the Bear's Paw Mountains in Montana.
On the morning of September 30, 1877, Chief Joseph prepared to break camp.
Sound of Running Water, help me ready the horses. We'll be leaving soon.
Yes, Father.
Father!
Soldiers!

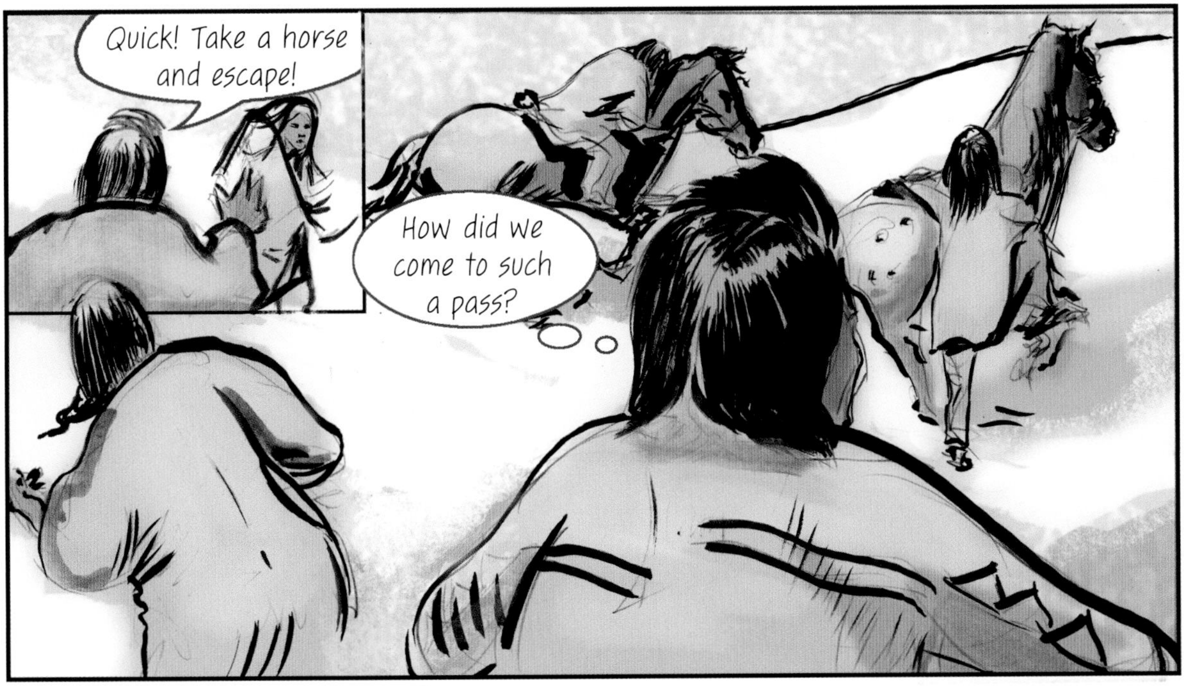
Quick! Take a horse and escape!
How did we come to such a pass?

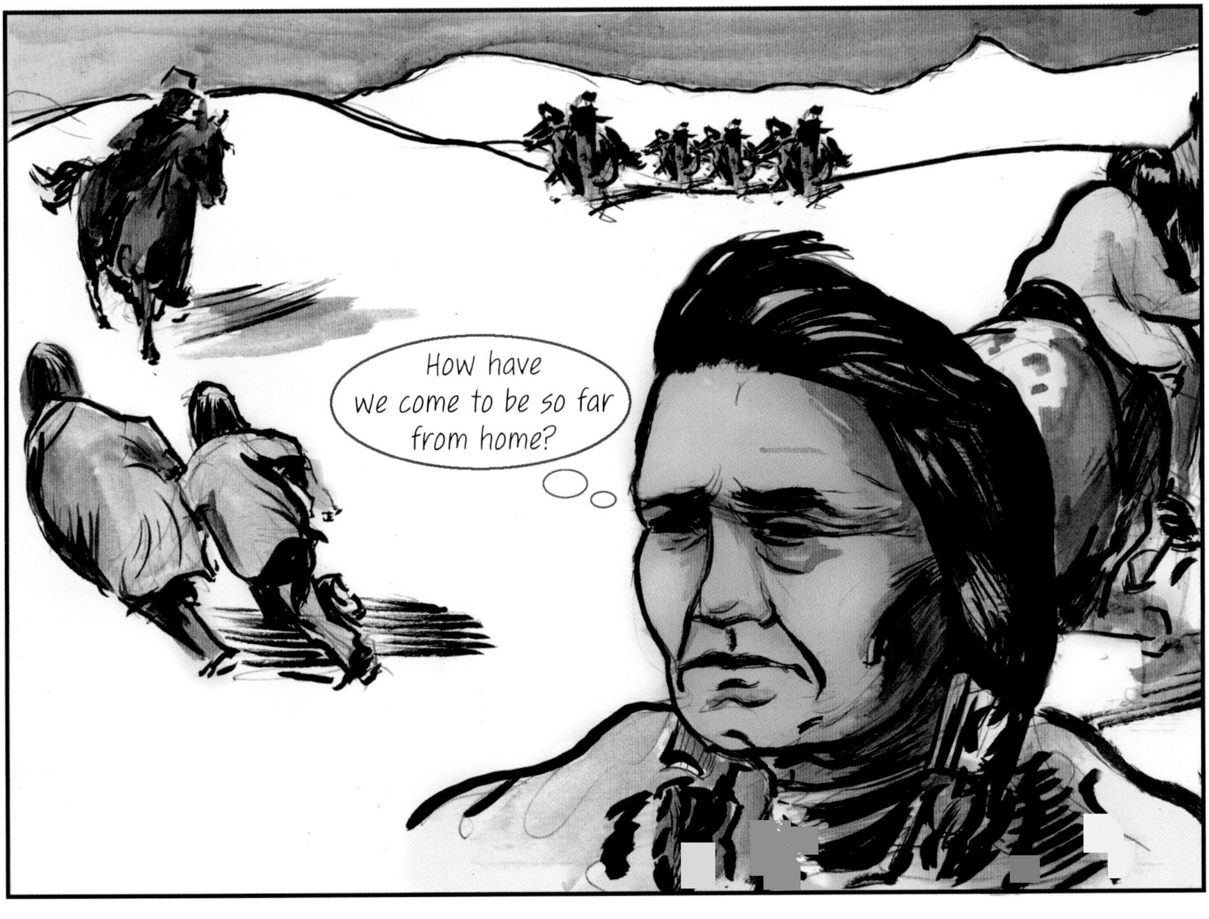
How have we come to be so far from home?

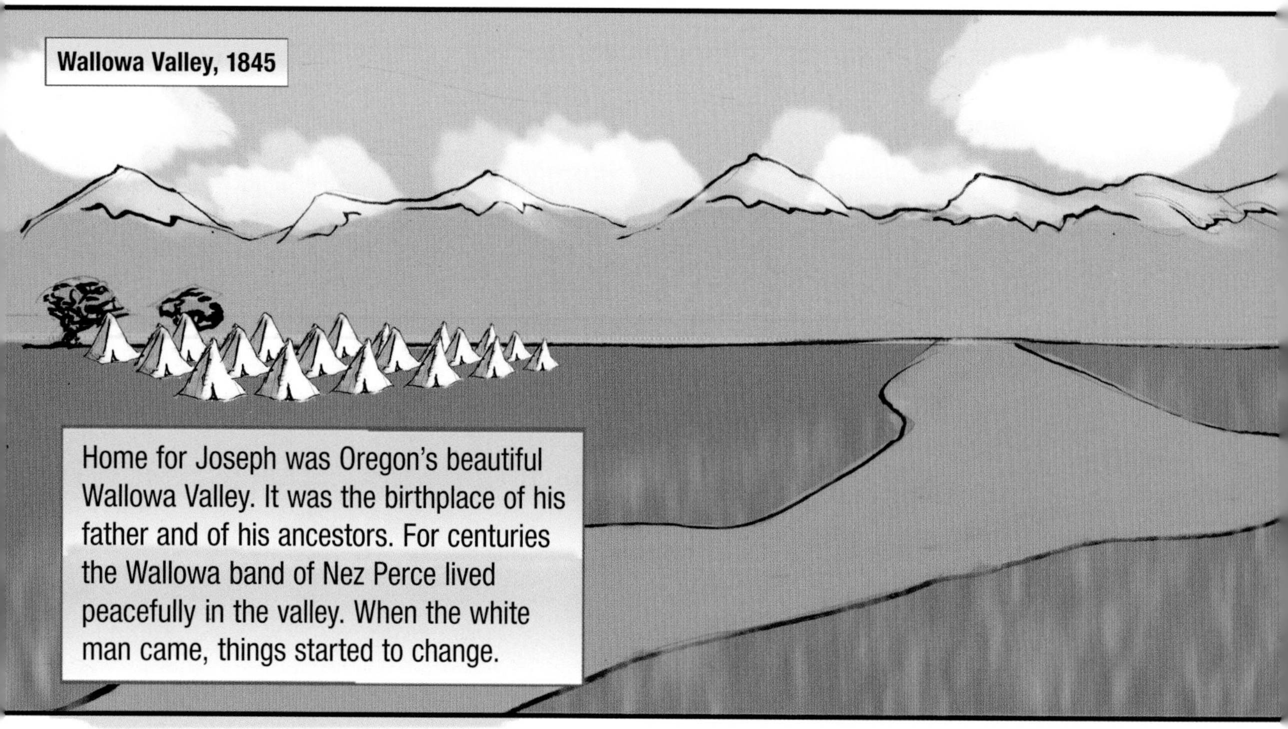
Wallowa Valley, 1845
Home for Joseph was Oregon's beautiful Wallowa Valley. It was the birthplace of his father and of his ancestors. For centuries the Wallowa band of Nez Perce lived peacefully in the valley. When the white man came, things started to change.

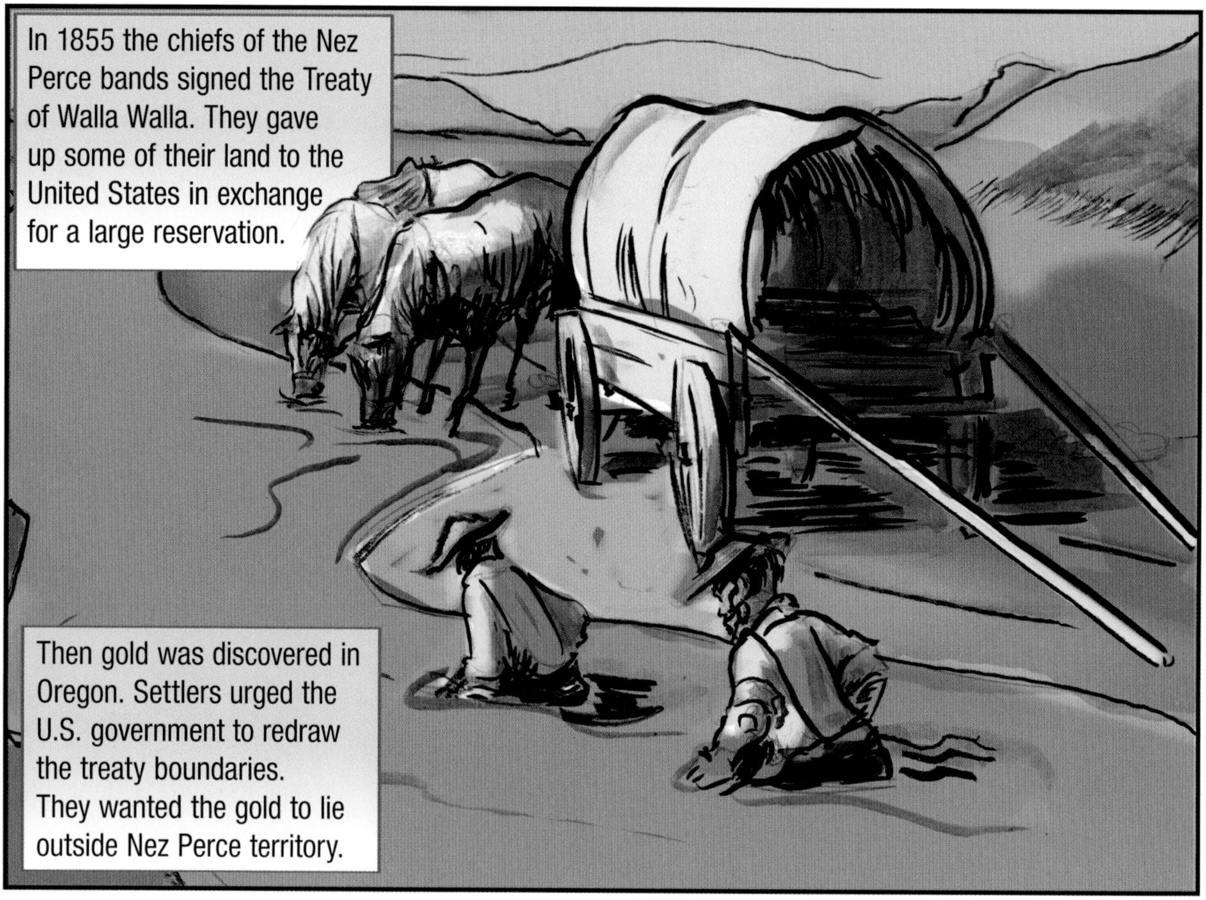
In 1855 the chiefs of the Nez Perce bands signed the Treaty of Walla Walla. They gave up some of their land to the United States in exchange for a large reservation.
Then gold was discovered in Oregon. Settlers urged the U.S. government to redraw the treaty boundaries. They wanted the gold to lie outside Nez Perce territory.

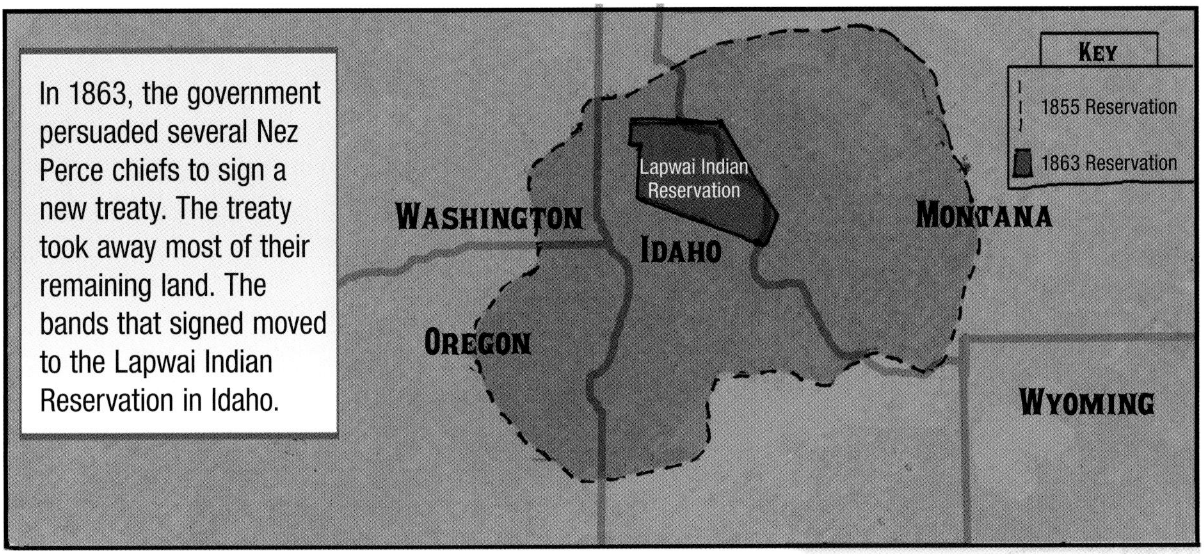
In 1863, the government persuaded several Nez Perce chiefs to sign a new treaty. The treaty took away most of their remaining land. The bands that signed moved to the Lapwai Indian Reservation in Idaho.
KEY
1855 Reservation
1863 Reservation
Lapwai Indian Reservation
WASHINGTON
IDAHO
MONTANA
OREGON
WYOMING

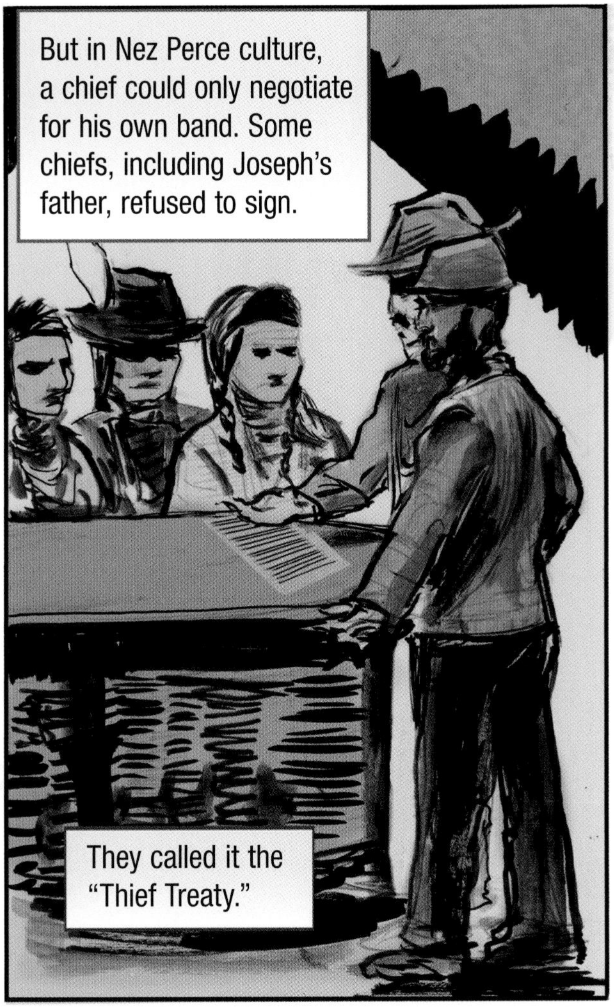
But in Nez Perce culture, a chief could only negotiate for his own band. Some chiefs, including Joseph's father, refused to sign.
They called it the "Thief Treaty."

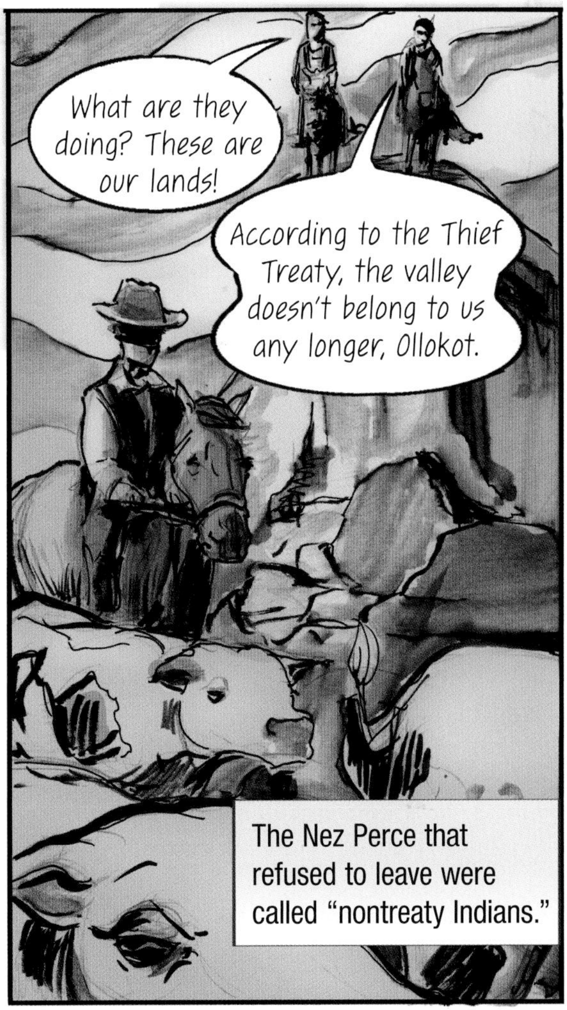
What are they doing? These are our lands!
According to the Thief Treaty, the valley doesn't belong to us any longer, Ollokot.
The Nez Perce that refused to leave were called "nontreaty Indians."

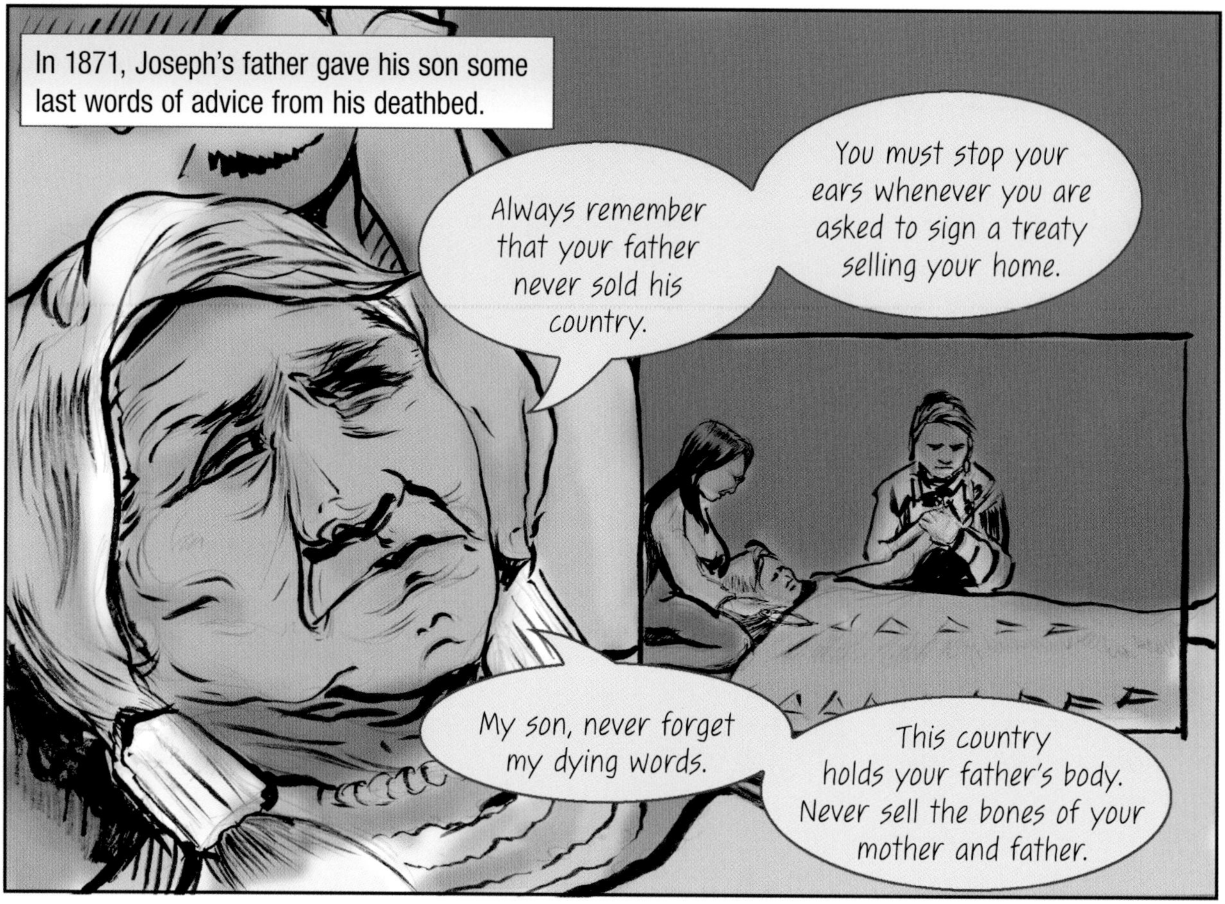
In 1871, Joseph's father gave his son some last words of advice from his deathbed.
Always remember that your father never sold his country.
You must stop your ears whenever you are asked to sign a treaty selling your home.
My son, never forget my dying words.
This country holds your father's body. Never sell the bones of your mother and father.

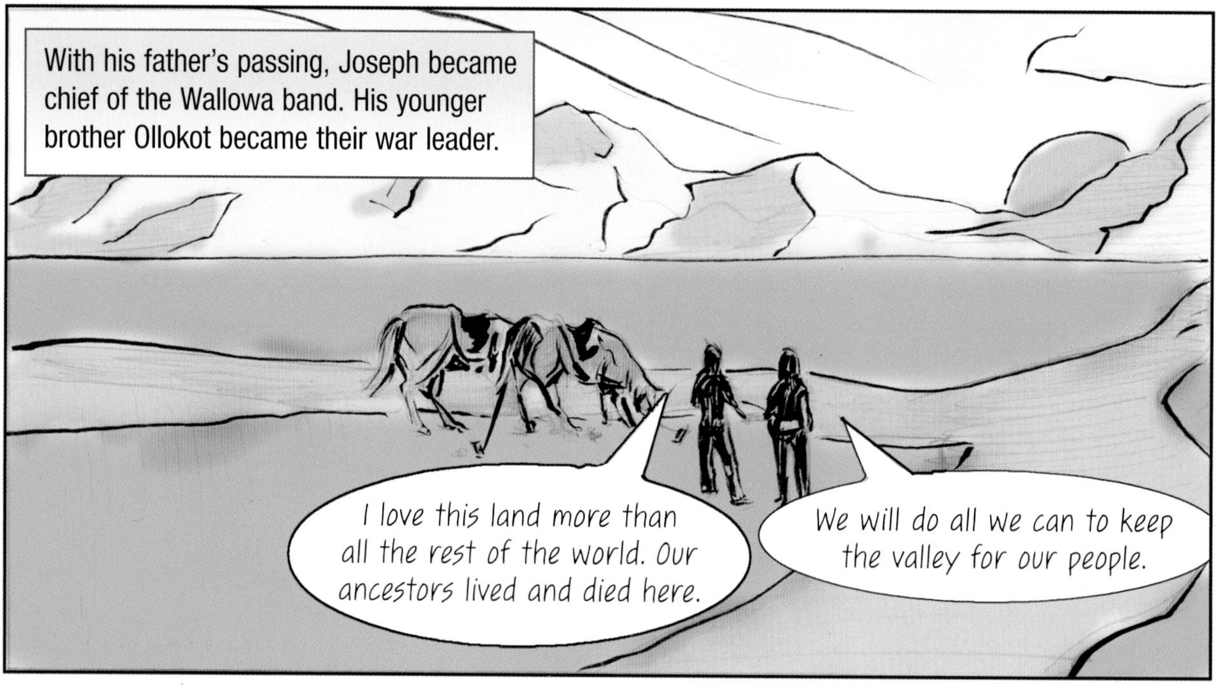
With his father's passing, Joseph became chief of the Wallowa band. His younger brother Ollokot became their war leader.
I love this land more than all the rest of the world. Our ancestors lived and died here.
We will do all we can to keep the valley for our people.

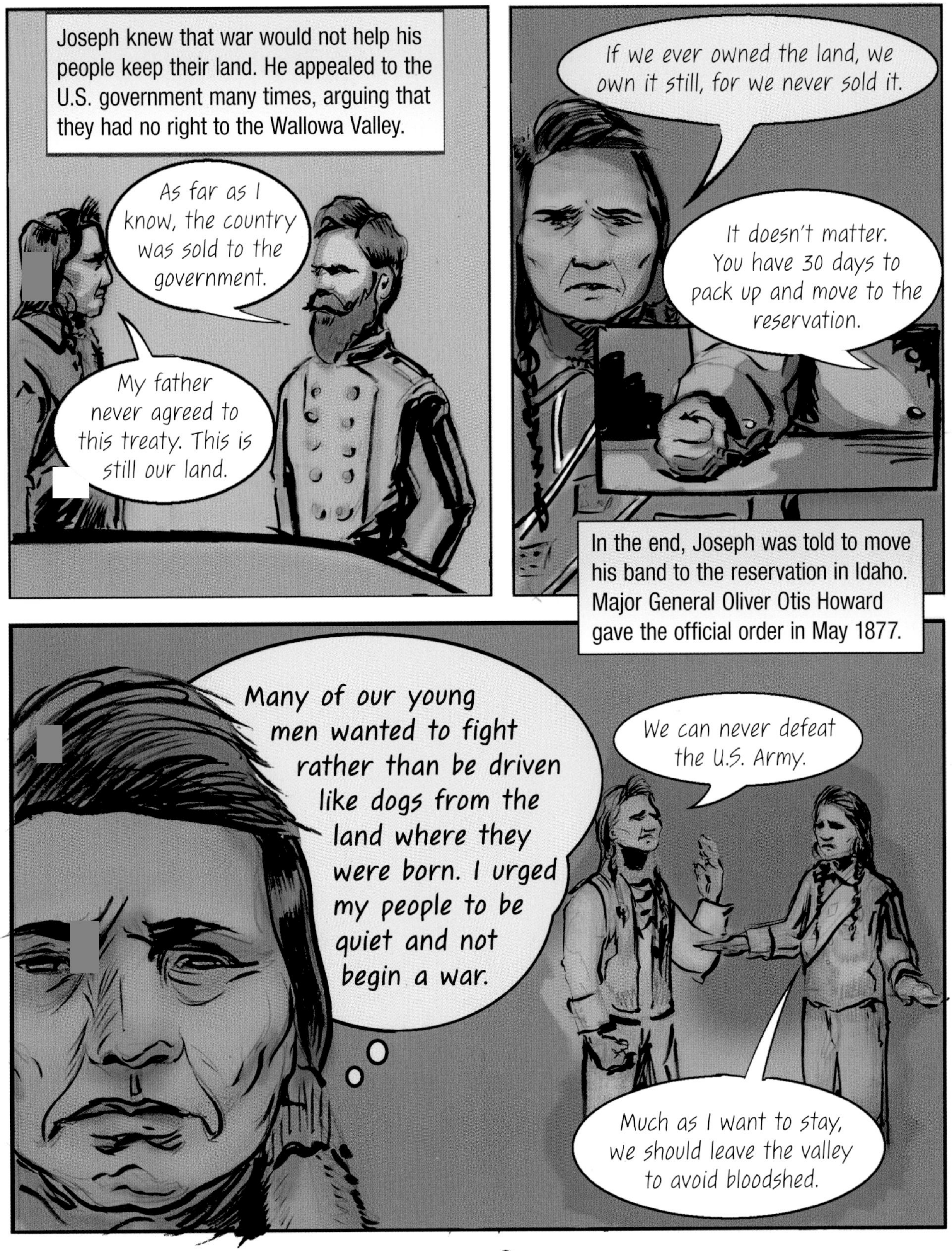
Joseph knew that war would not help his people keep their land. He appealed to the U.S. government many times, arguing that they had no right to the Wallowa Valley.
As far as I know, the country was sold to the government.
My father never agreed to this treaty. This is still our land.
If we ever owned the land, we own it still, for we never sold it.
It doesn't matter. You have 30 days to pack up and move to the reservation.
In the end, Joseph was told to move his band to the reservation in Idaho. Major General Oliver Otis Howard gave the official order in May 1877.
Many of our young men wanted to fight rather than be driven like dogs from the land where they were born. I urged my people to be quiet and not begin a war.
We can never defeat the U.S. Army.
Much as I want to stay, we should leave the valley to avoid bloodshed.

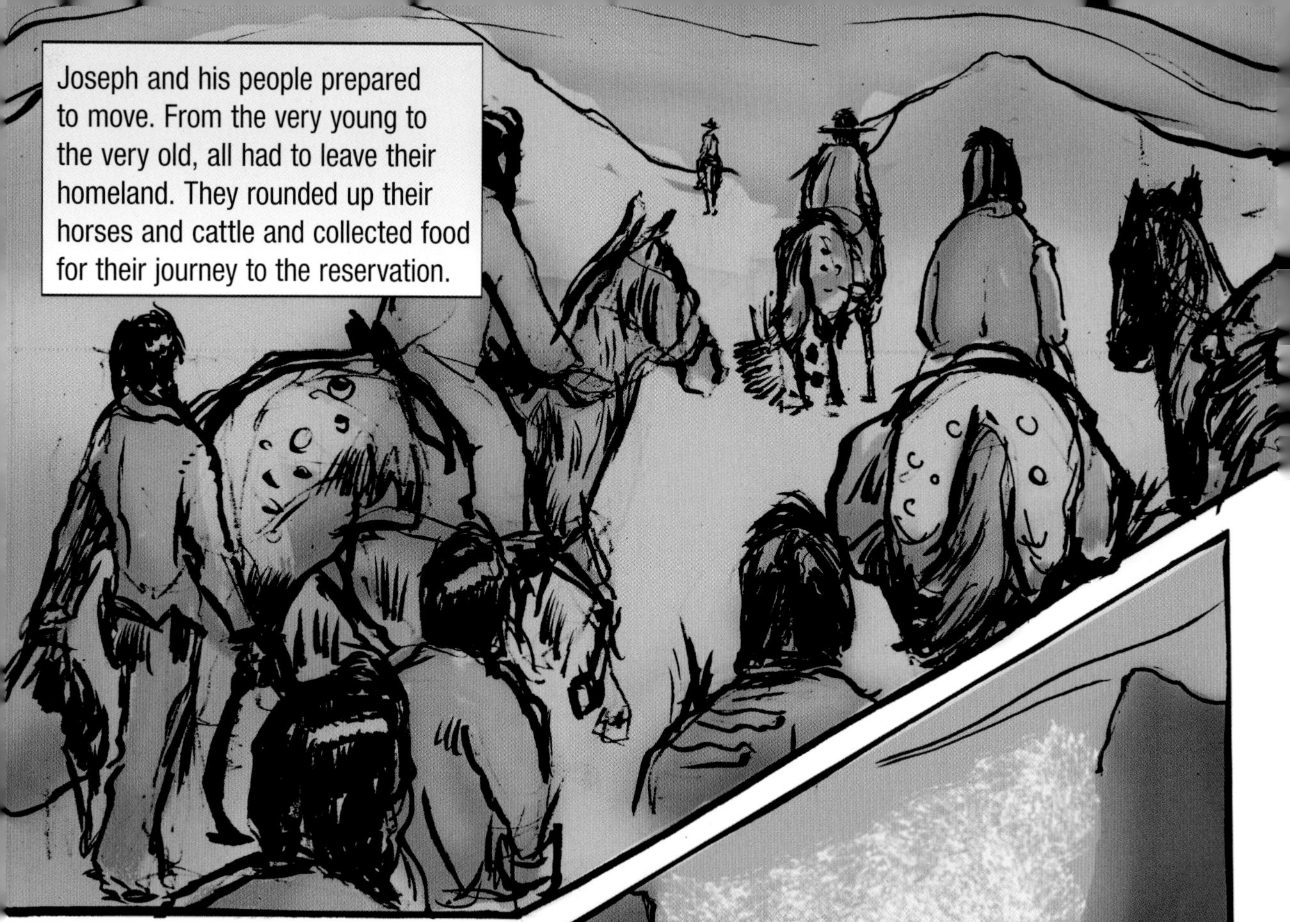
Joseph and his people prepared to move. From the very young to the very old, all had to leave their homeland. They rounded up their horses and cattle and collected food for their journey to the reservation.

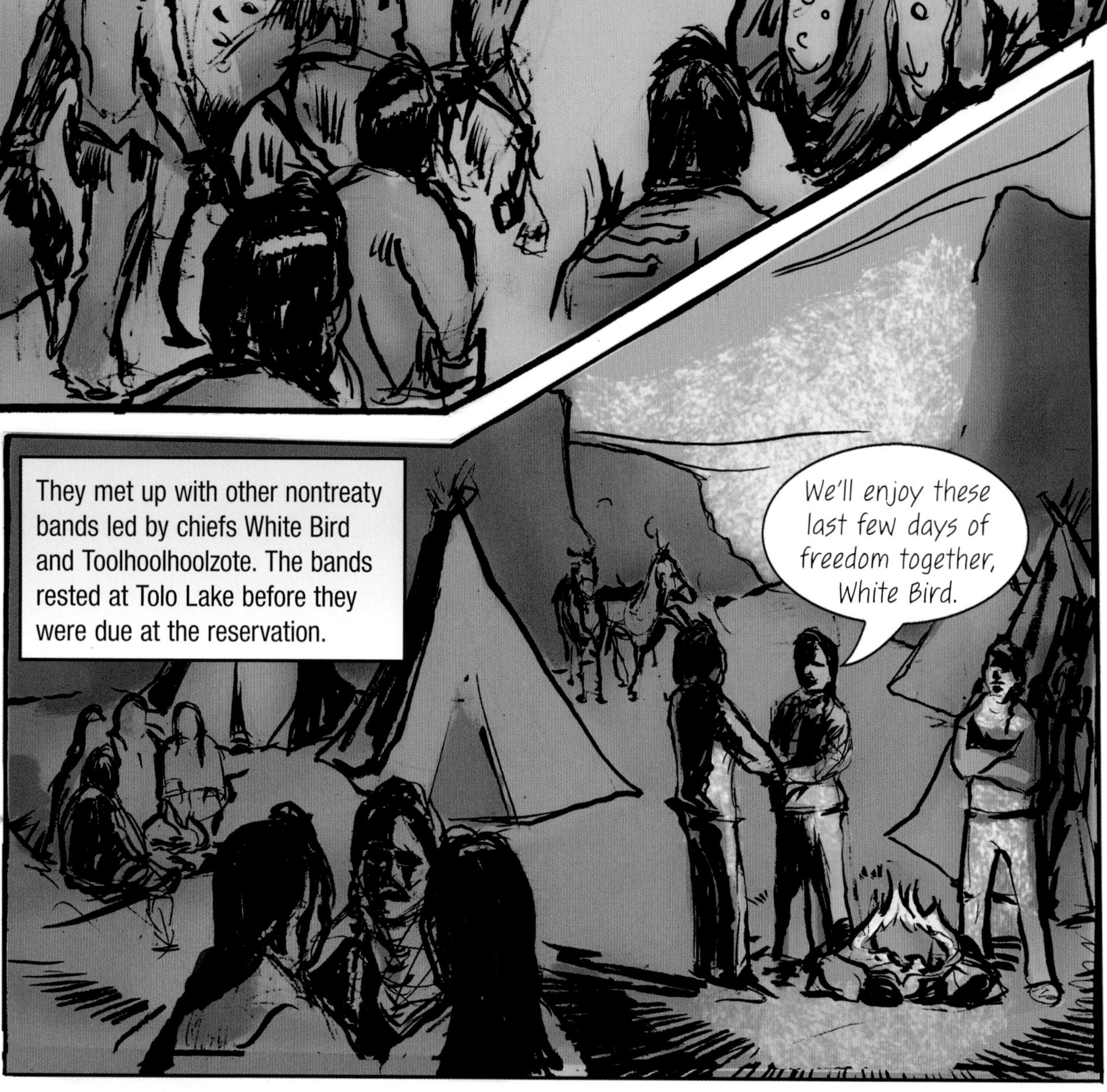
They met up with other nontreaty bands led by chiefs White Bird and Toolhoolhoolzote. The bands rested at Tolo Lake before they were due at the reservation.
We'll enjoy these last few days of freedom together, White Bird.

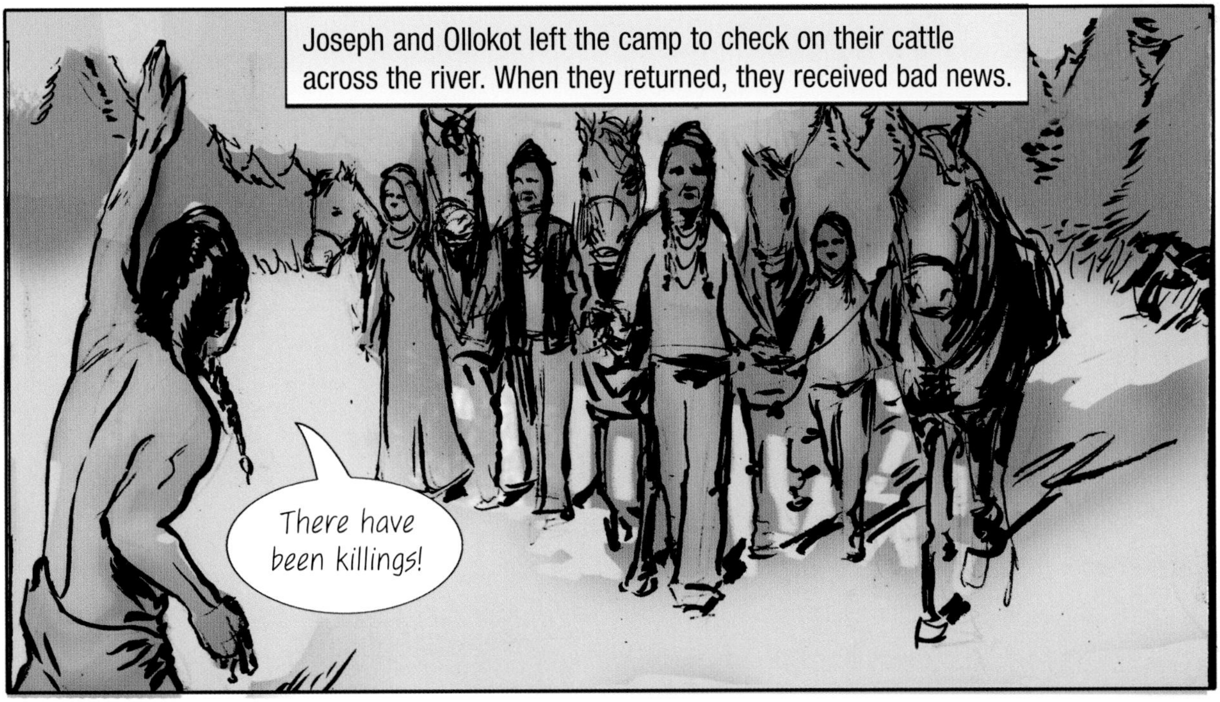
Joseph and Ollokot left the camp to check on their cattle across the river. When they returned, they received bad news.
There have been killings!

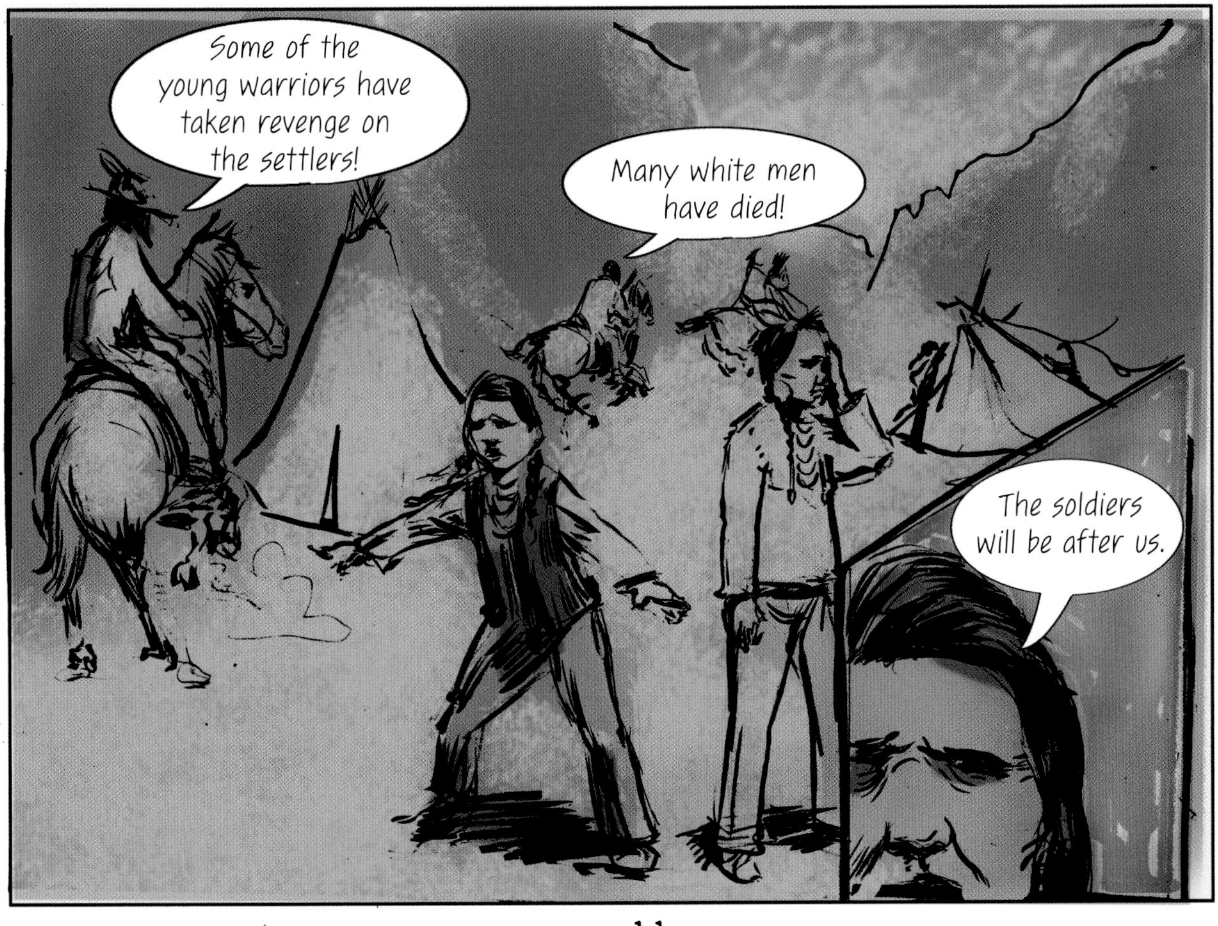
Some of the young warriors have taken revenge on the settlers!
Many white men have died!
The soldiers will be after us.

CHAPTER 2 FIGHT

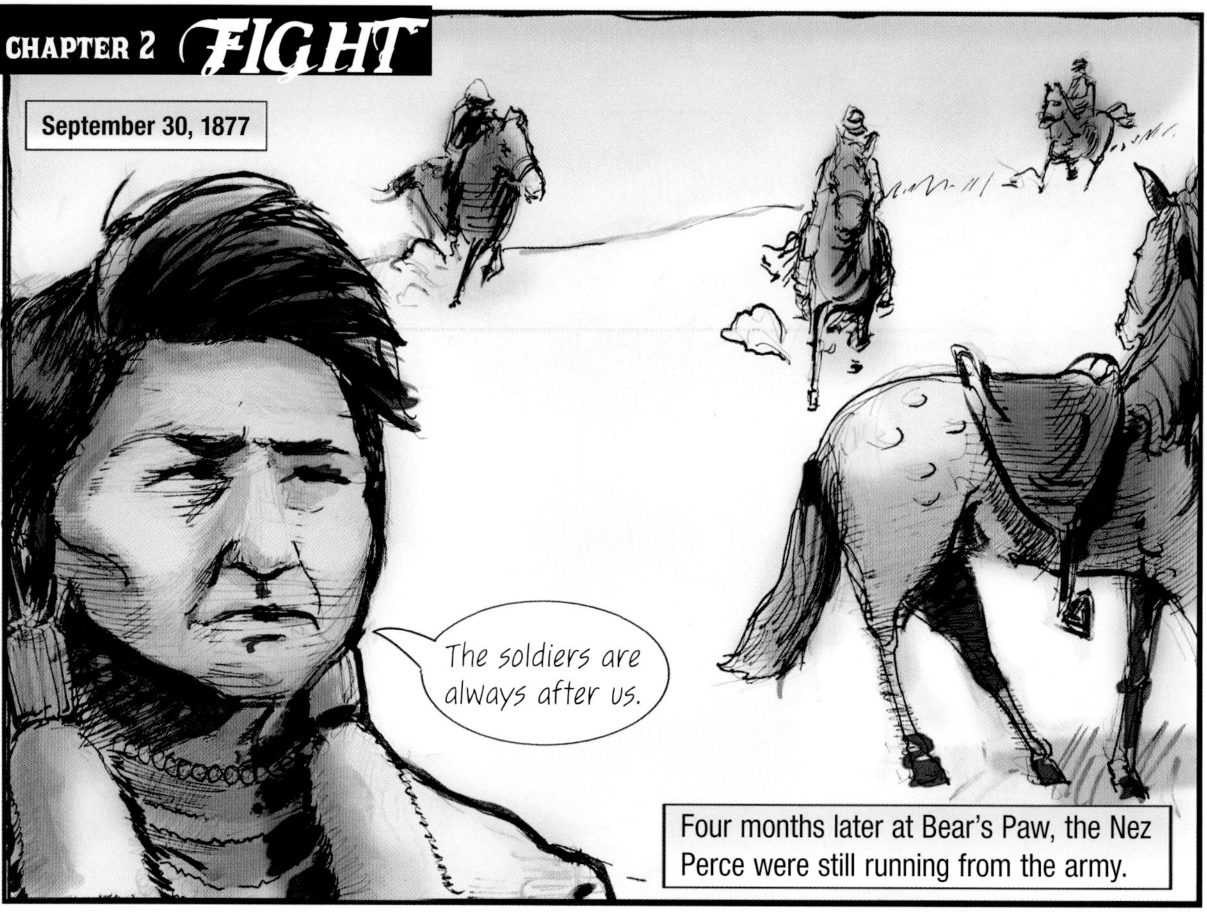
September 30, 1877
The soldiers are always after us.
Four months later at Bear's Paw, the Nez Perce were still running from the army.

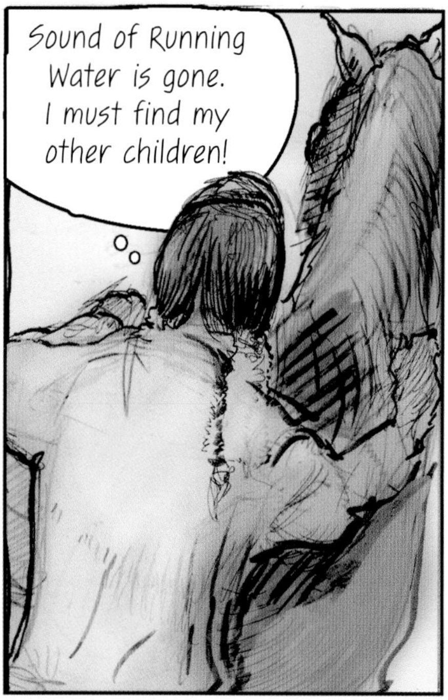
Sound of Running Water is gone. I must find my other children!

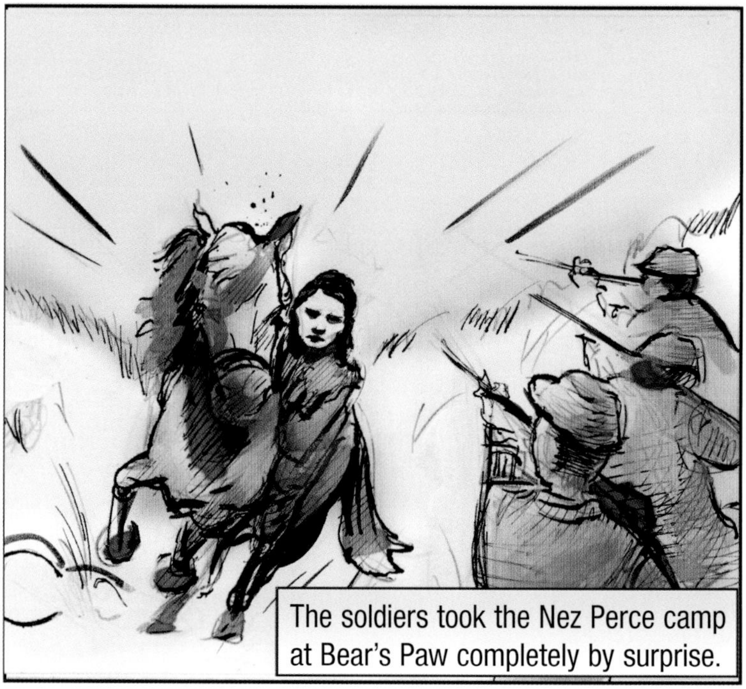
The soldiers took the Nez Perce camp at Bear's Paw completely by surprise.

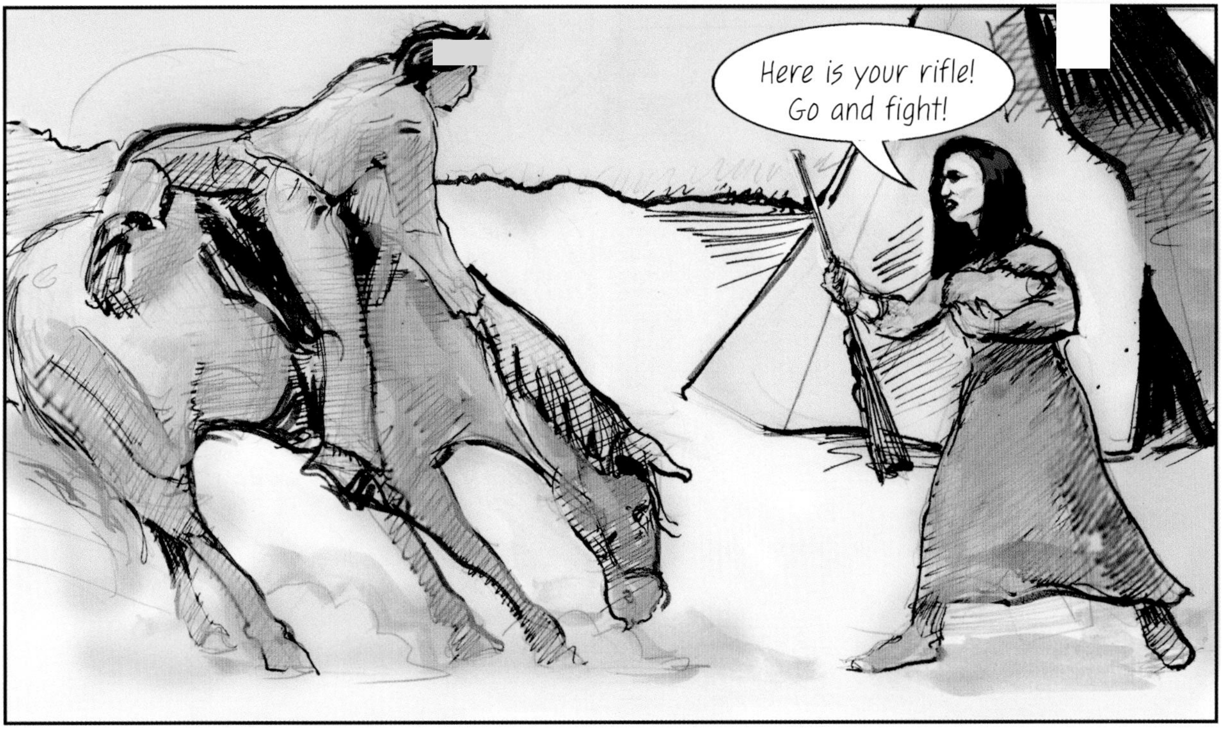
Here is your rifle! Go and fight!

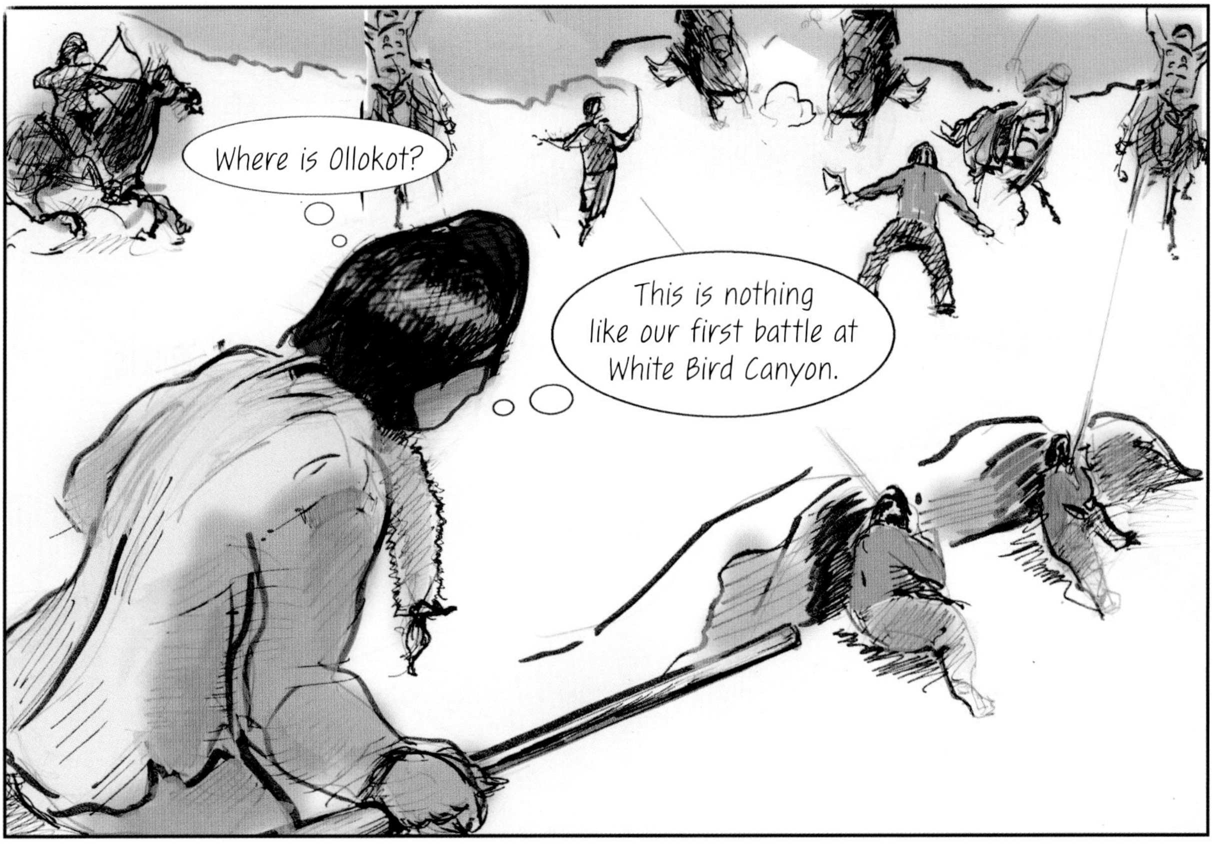
Where is Ollokot?
This is nothing like our first battle at White Bird Canyon.

June 1877

After the settlers were killed, Joseph knew they had no choice but to run. They met with other nontreaty Nez Perce at White Bird Canyon.

The soldiers will find us soon. The canyon should help protect us from a surprise attack.

We should talk with them. Peace may still be possible.

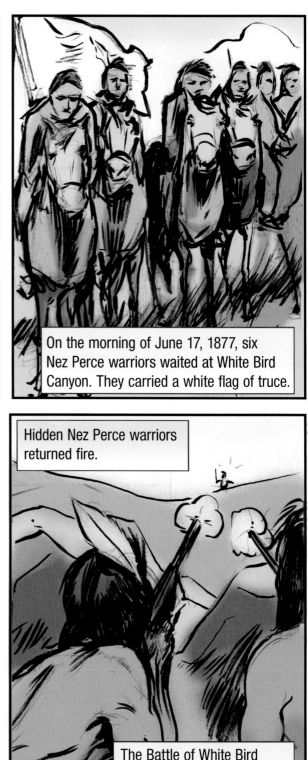

On the morning of June 17, 1877, six Nez Perce warriors waited at White Bird Canyon. They carried a white flag of truce.

One of the soldiers fired shots at the Nez Perce.

Hidden Nez Perce warriors returned fire.

The Battle of White Bird Canyon—the first battle of the Nez Perce War—had begun.

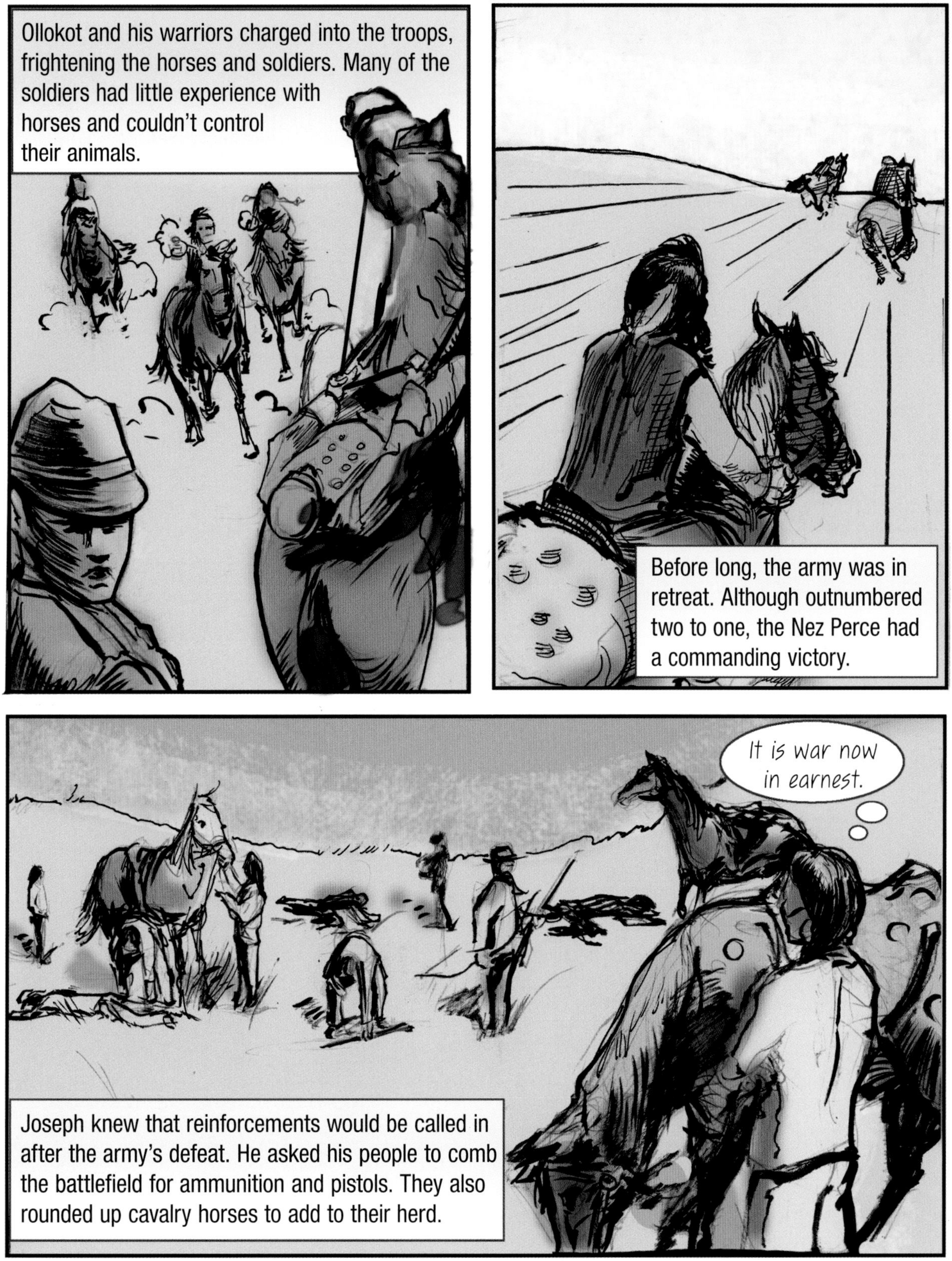
Ollokot and his warriors charged into the troops, frightening the horses and soldiers. Many of the soldiers had little experience with horses and couldn't control their animals.
Before long, the army was in retreat. Although outnumbered two to one, the Nez Perce had a commanding victory.
It is war now in earnest.
Joseph knew that reinforcements would be called in after the army's defeat. He asked his people to comb the battlefield for ammunition and pistols. They also rounded up cavalry horses to add to their herd.

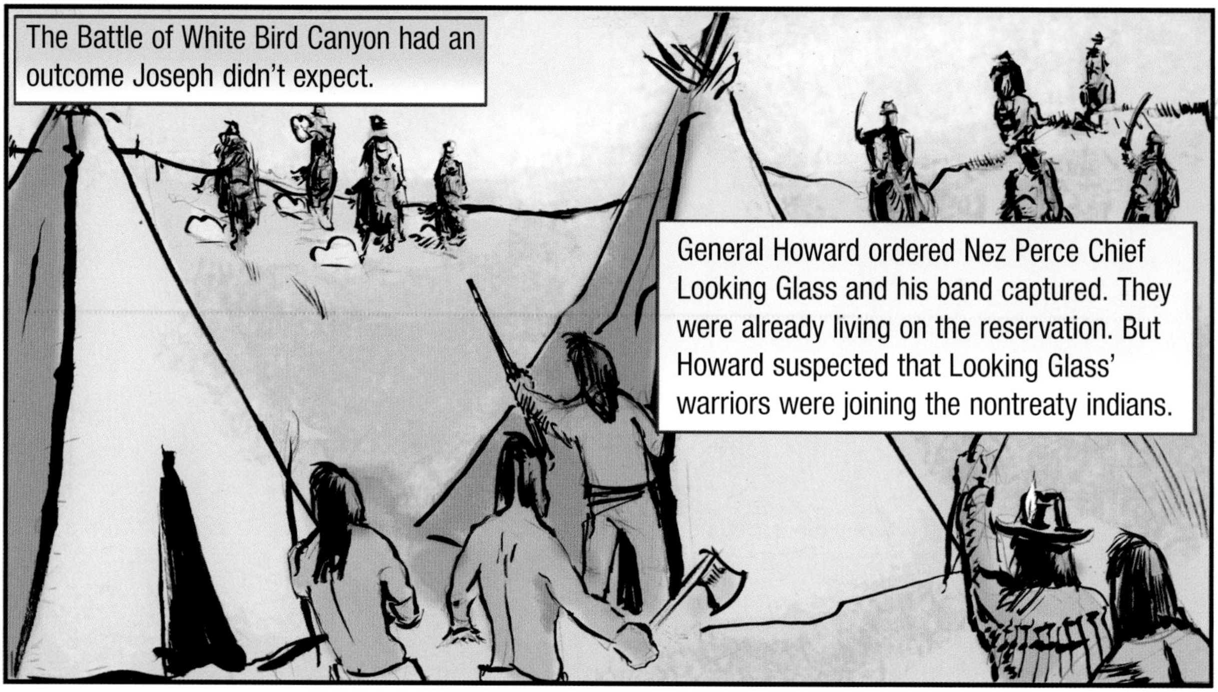
The Battle of White Bird Canyon had an outcome Joseph didn't expect.
General Howard ordered Nez Perce Chief Looking Glass and his band captured. They were already living on the reservation. But Howard suspected that Looking Glass' warriors were joining the nontreaty indians.

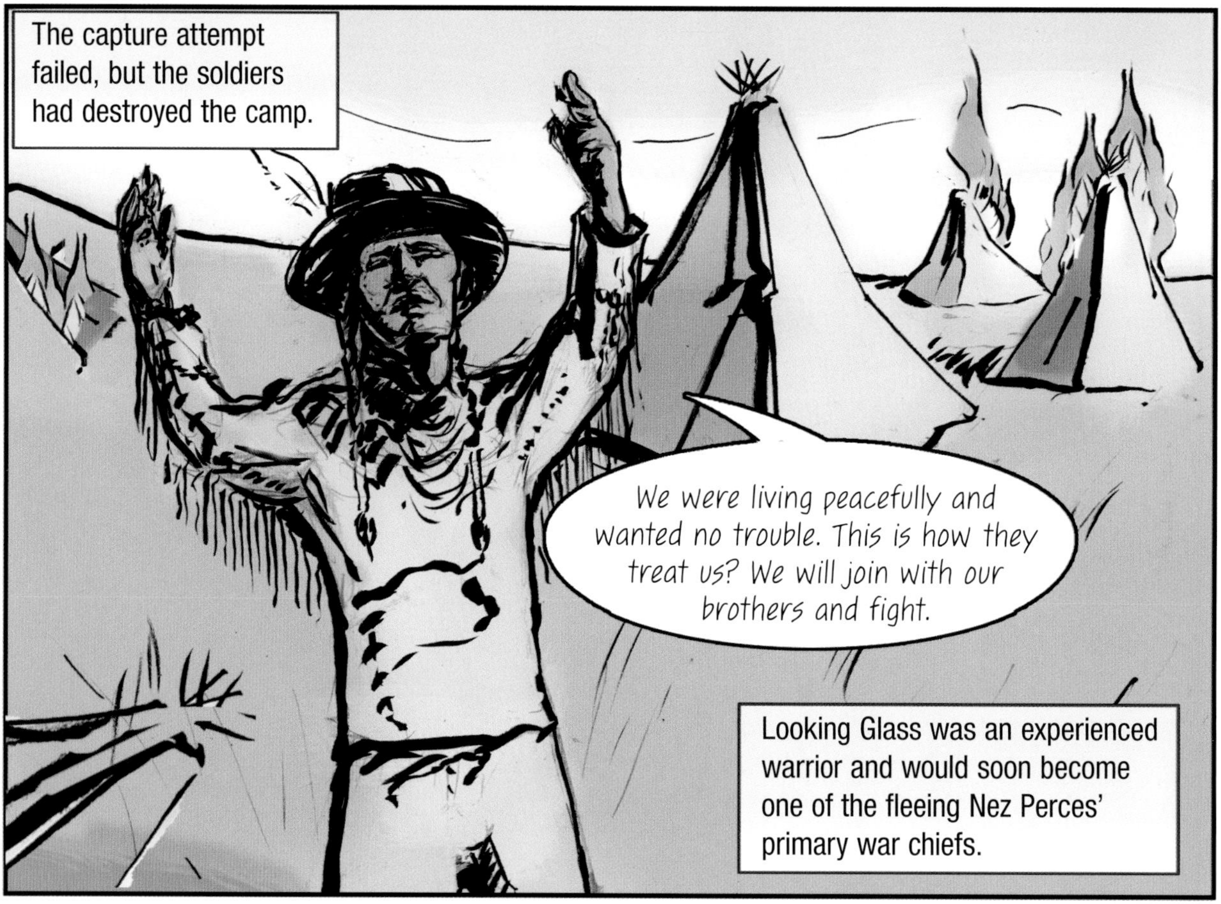
The capture attempt failed, but the soldiers had destroyed the camp.
We were living peacefully and wanted no trouble. This is how they treat us? We will join with our brothers and fight.
Looking Glass was an experienced warrior and would soon become one of the fleeing Nez Perces' primary war chiefs.

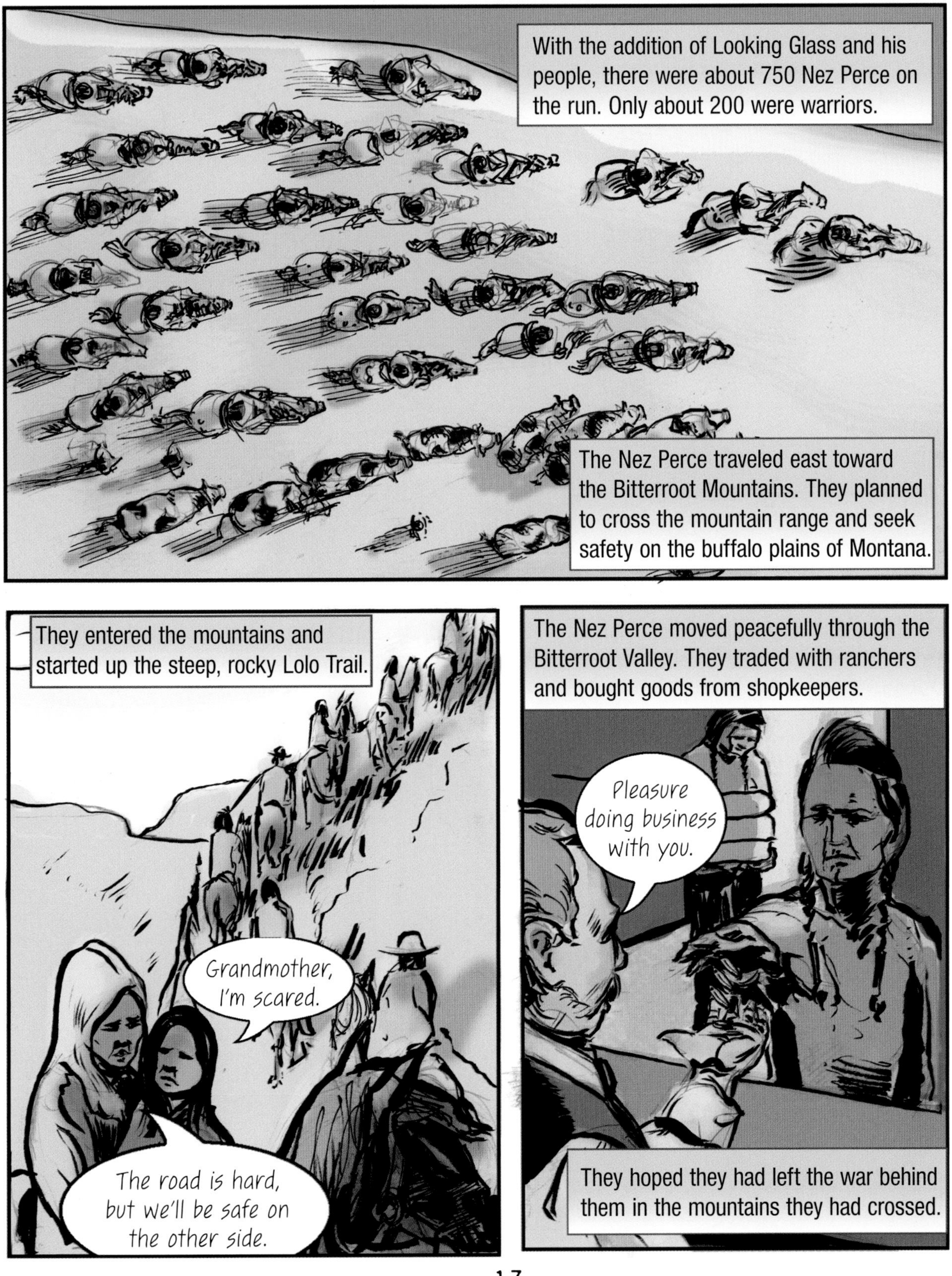
With the addition of Looking Glass and his people, there were about 750 Nez Perce on the run. Only about 200 were warriors.
The Nez Perce traveled east toward the Bitterroot Mountains. They planned to cross the mountain range and seek safety on the buffalo plains of Montana.
They entered the mountains and started up the steep, rocky Lolo Trail.
Grandmother, I'm scared.
The road is hard, but we'll be safe on the other side.
The Nez Perce moved peacefully through the Bitterroot Valley. They traded with ranchers and bought goods from shopkeepers.
Pleasure doing business with you.
They hoped they had left the war behind them in the mountains they had crossed.

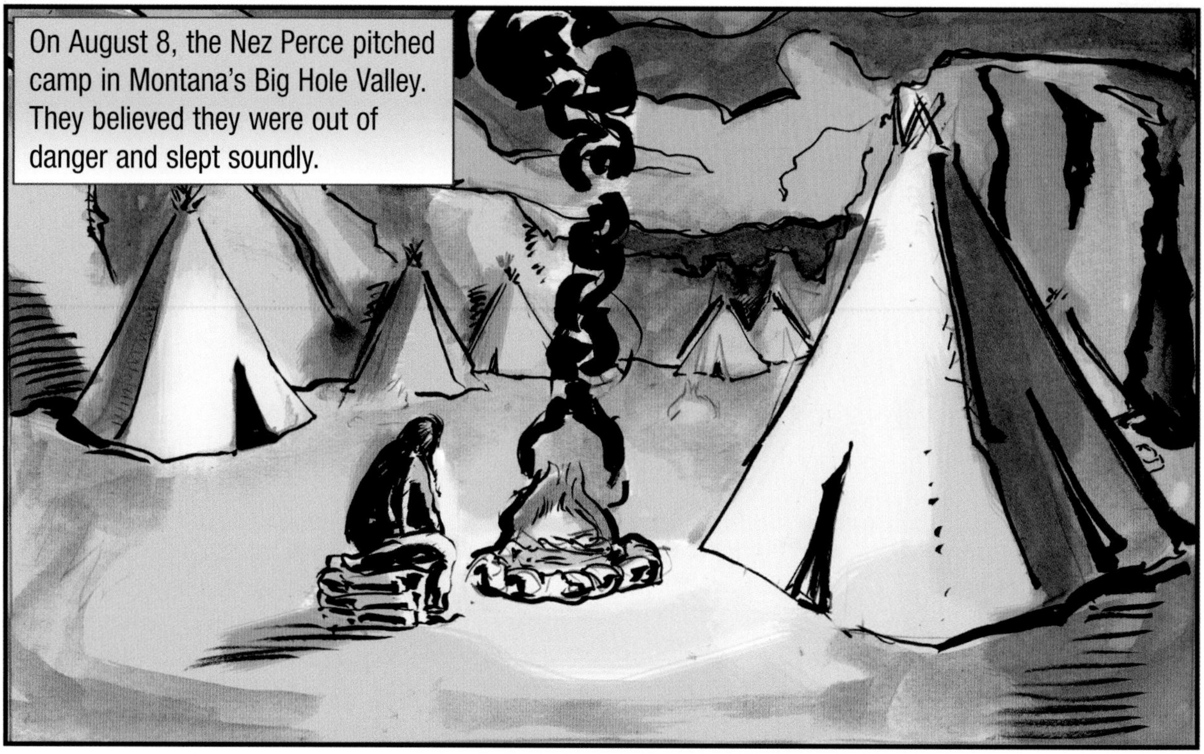
On August 8, the Nez Perce pitched camp in Montana's Big Hole Valley. They believed they were out of danger and slept soundly.

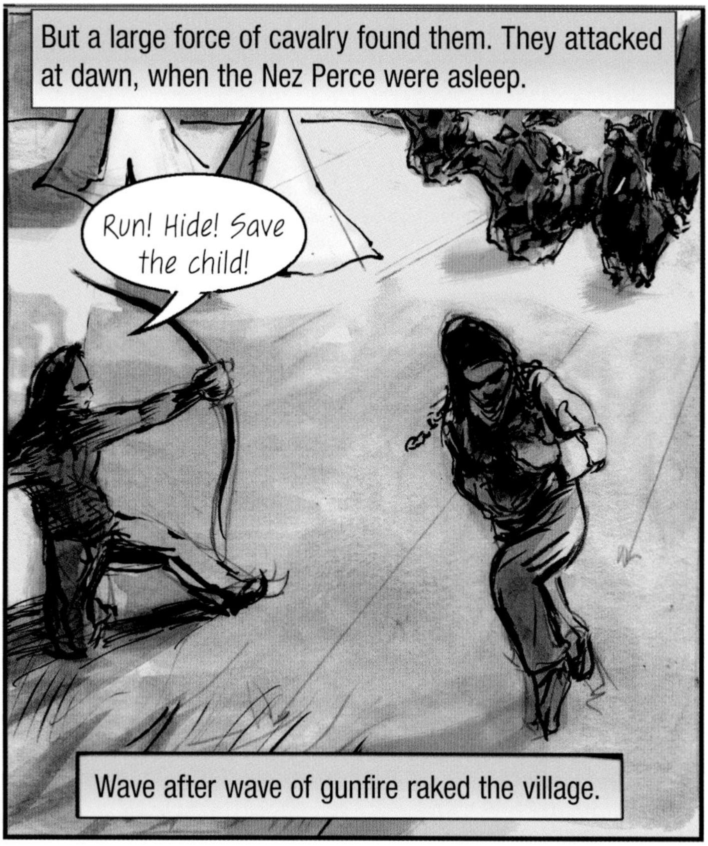
But a large force of cavalry found them. They attacked at dawn, when the Nez Perce were asleep.
Run! Hide! Save the child!
Wave after wave of gunfire raked the village.

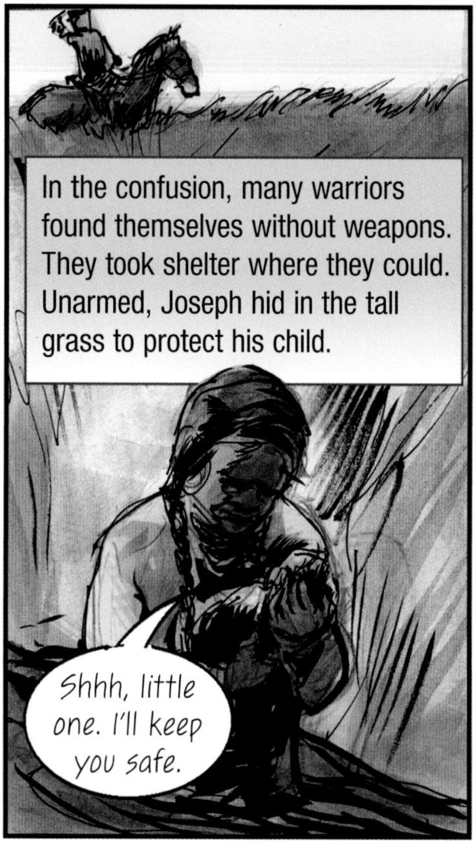
In the confusion, many warriors found themselves without weapons. They took shelter where they could. Unarmed, Joseph hid in the tall grass to protect his child.
Shhh, little one. I'll keep you safe.

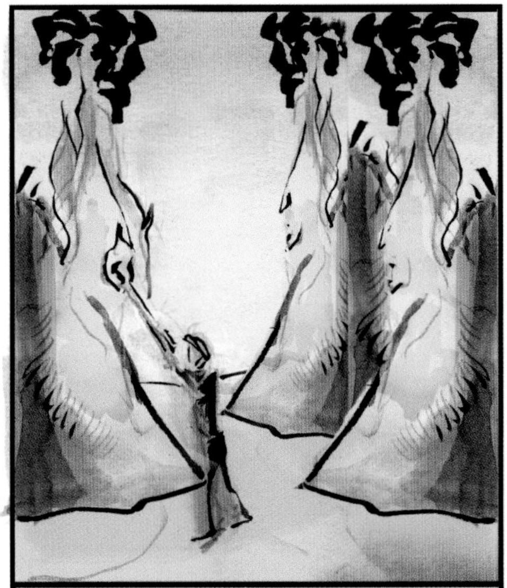

Not everyone was so lucky. Many people were mowed down by gunfire. Soldiers set the mat lodges on fire. Women and children were killed.

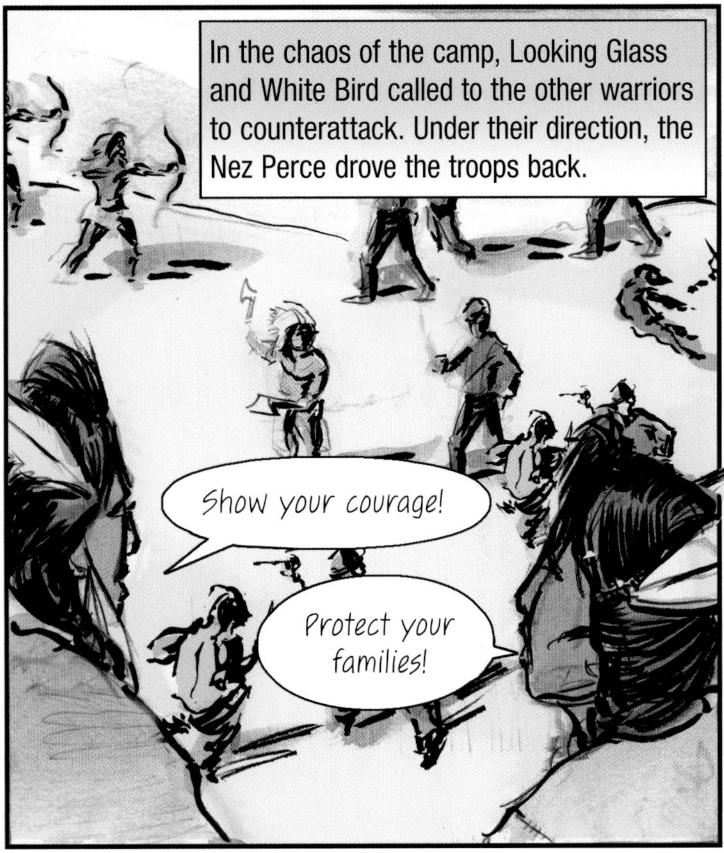
In the chaos of the camp, Looking Glass and White Bird called to the other warriors to counterattack. Under their direction, the Nez Perce drove the troops back.
Show your courage!
Protect your families!

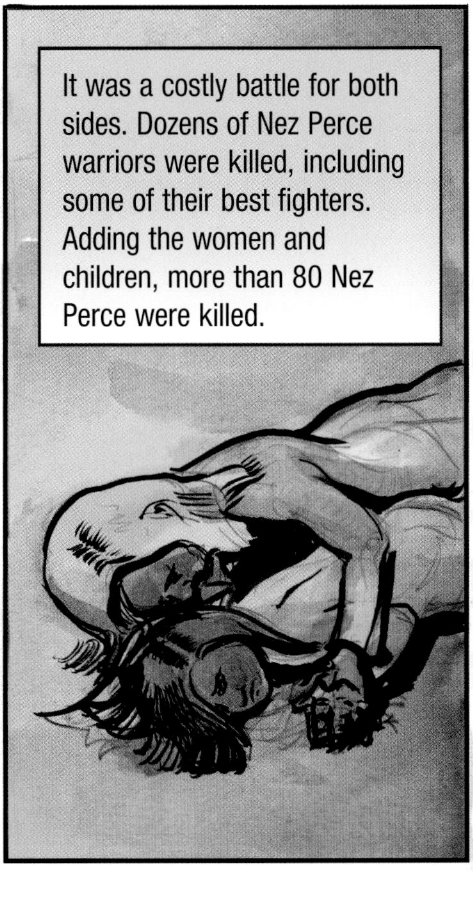
It was a costly battle for both sides. Dozens of Nez Perce warriors were killed, including some of their best fighters. Adding the women and children, more than 80 Nez Perce were killed.

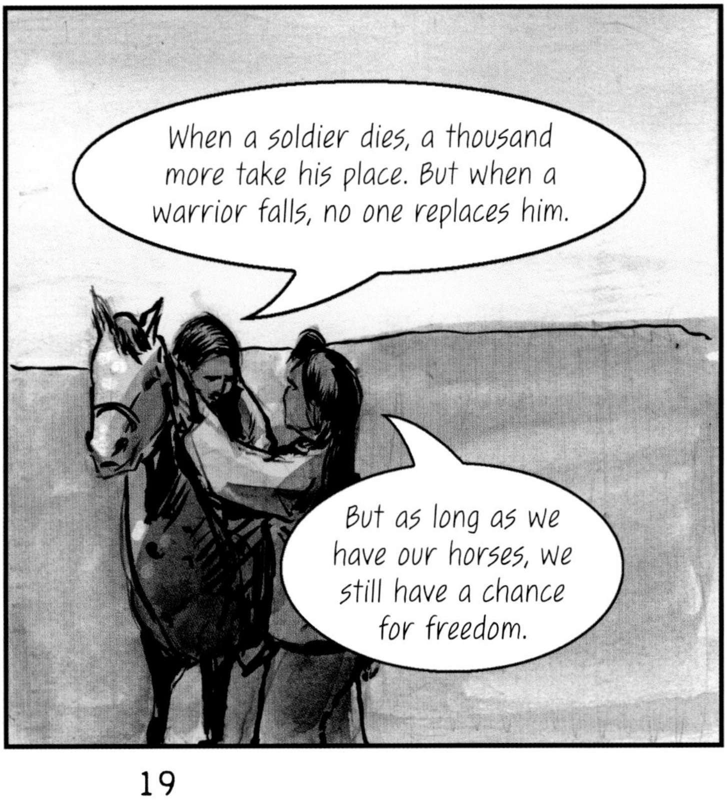
When a soldier dies, a thousand more take his place. But when a warrior falls, no one replaces him.
But as long as we have our horses, we still have a chance for freedom.

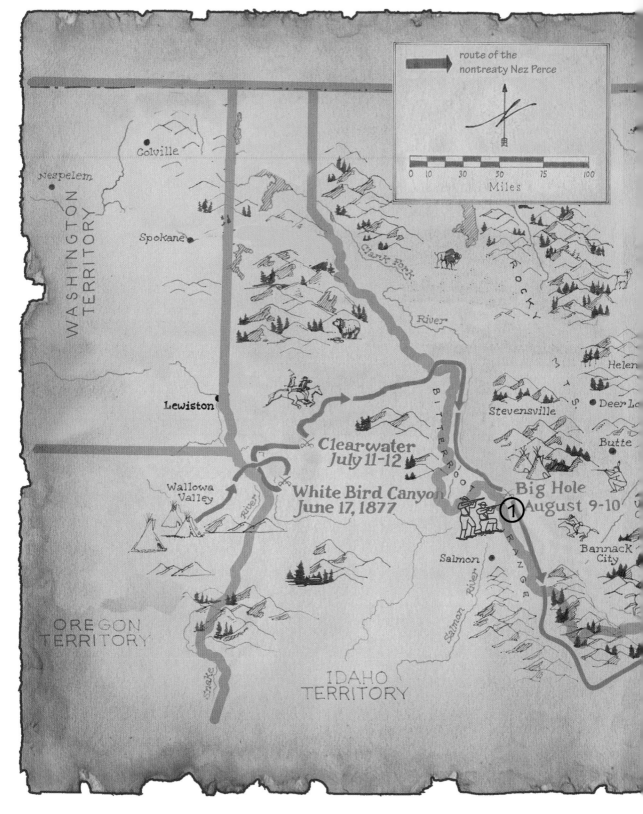

route of the
nontreaty Nez Perce

0 10 30 30 75 100
Miles

WASHINGTON TERRITORY

Nespelem

Colville

Spokane

Lewiston

Wallowa
Valley

OREGON
TERRITORY

IDAHO
TERRITORY

Snake River

Clearwater
July 11-12

White Bird Canyon
June 17, 1877

Salmon

Salmon River

Clark Fork

River

ROCKY

BITTERROOT

Stevensville

Helen

Deer Lo

Butte

Big Hole
August 9-10

Bannack
City

①

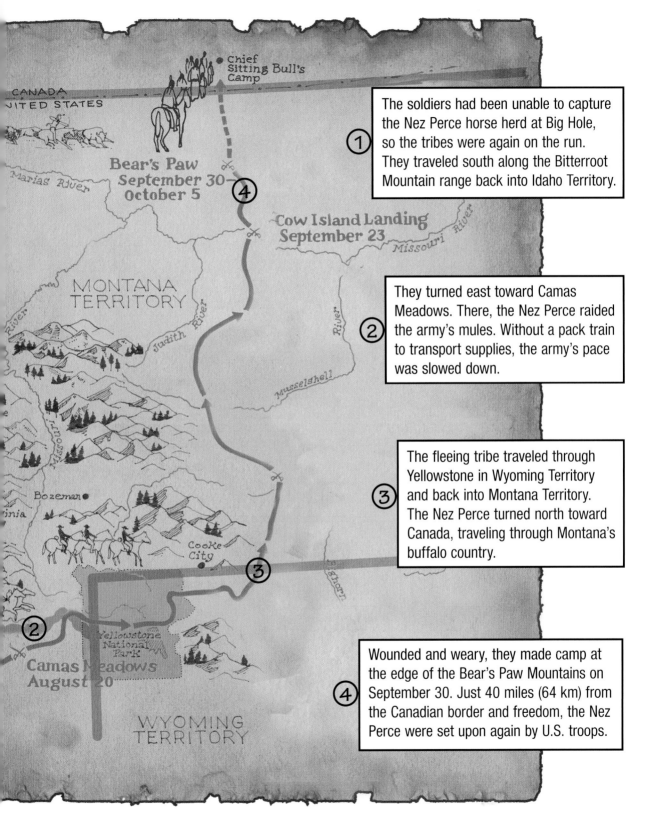

Chief Sitting Bull's Camp

CANADA
UNITED STATES

Bear's Paw
September 30–
October 5
④

Cow Island Landing
September 23

Missouri River

Marias River

MONTANA
TERRITORY

Judith River

River

Musselshell

Bozeman

inia

Cooke City

③

Yellowstone National Park

②
Camas Meadows
August 20

WYOMING
TERRITORY

① The soldiers had been unable to capture the Nez Perce horse herd at Big Hole, so the tribes were again on the run. They traveled south along the Bitterroot Mountain range back into Idaho Territory.

② They turned east toward Camas Meadows. There, the Nez Perce raided the army's mules. Without a pack train to transport supplies, the army's pace was slowed down.

③ The fleeing tribe traveled through Yellowstone in Wyoming Territory and back into Montana Territory. The Nez Perce turned north toward Canada, traveling through Montana's buffalo country.

④ Wounded and weary, they made camp at the edge of the Bear's Paw Mountains on September 30. Just 40 miles (64 km) from the Canadian border and freedom, the Nez Perce were set upon again by U.S. troops.

CHAPTER 3 SURRENDER

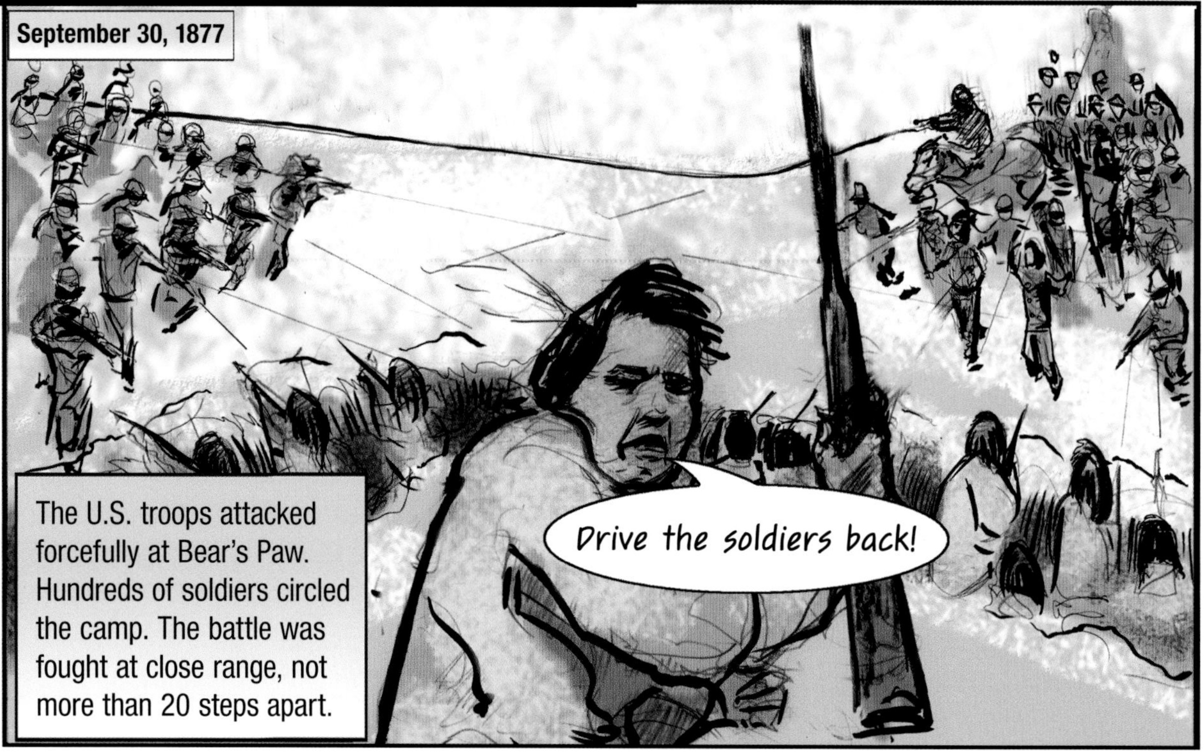
September 30, 1877
The U.S. troops attacked forcefully at Bear's Paw. Hundreds of soldiers circled the camp. The battle was fought at close range, not more than 20 steps apart.
Drive the soldiers back!

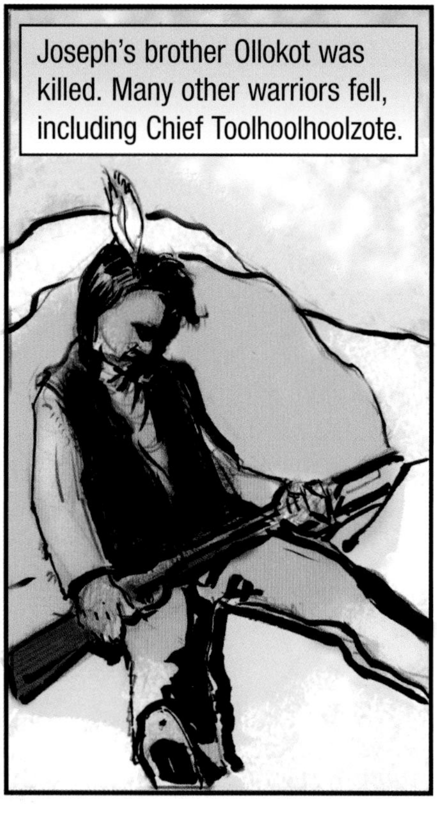
Joseph's brother Ollokot was killed. Many other warriors fell, including Chief Toolhoolhoolzote.

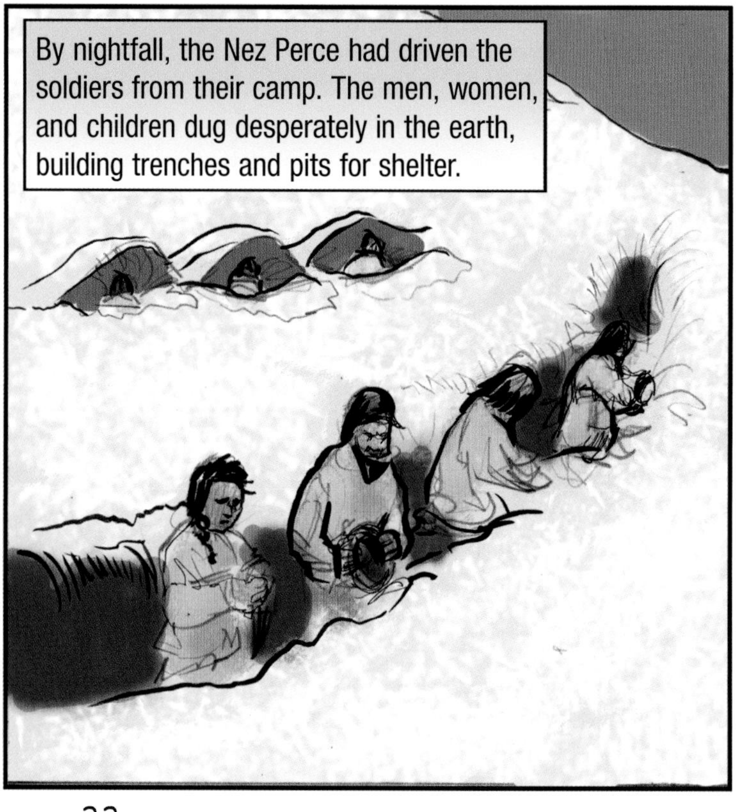
By nightfall, the Nez Perce had driven the soldiers from their camp. The men, women, and children dug desperately in the earth, building trenches and pits for shelter.

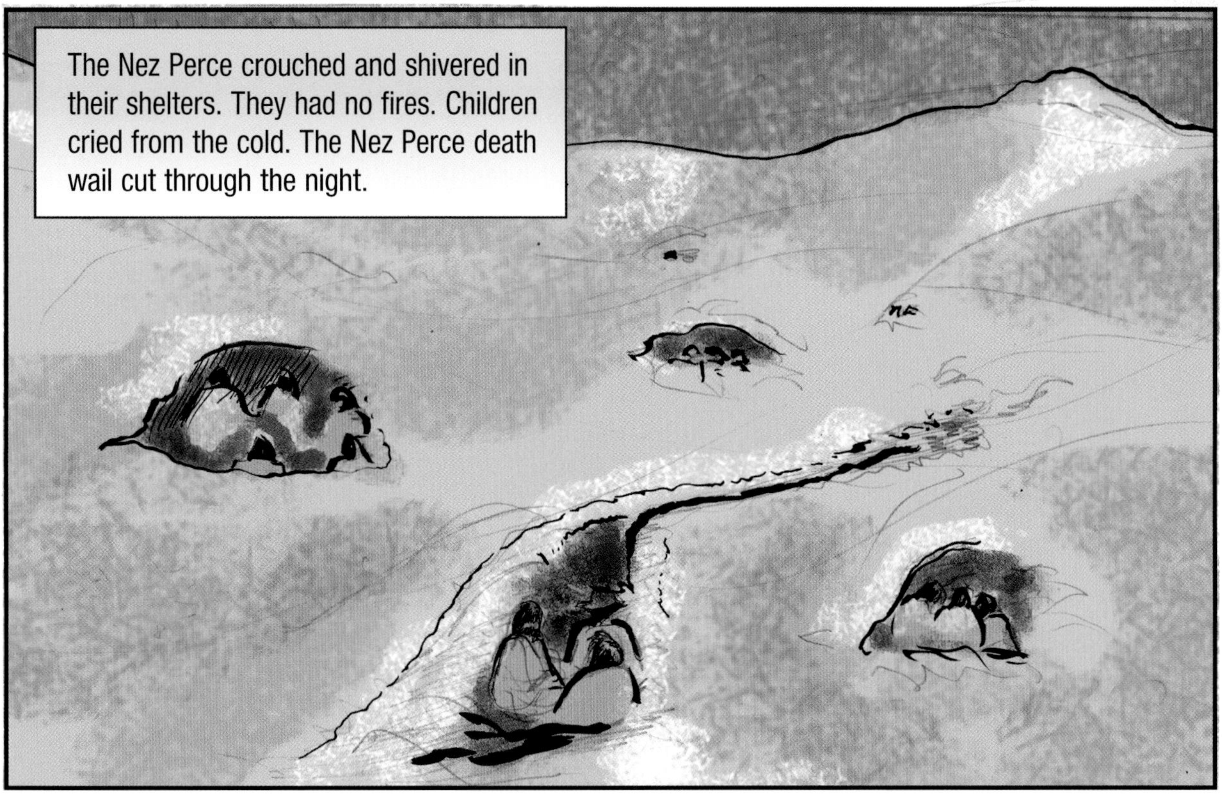

The Nez Perce crouched and shivered in their shelters. They had no fires. Children cried from the cold. The Nez Perce death wail cut through the night.

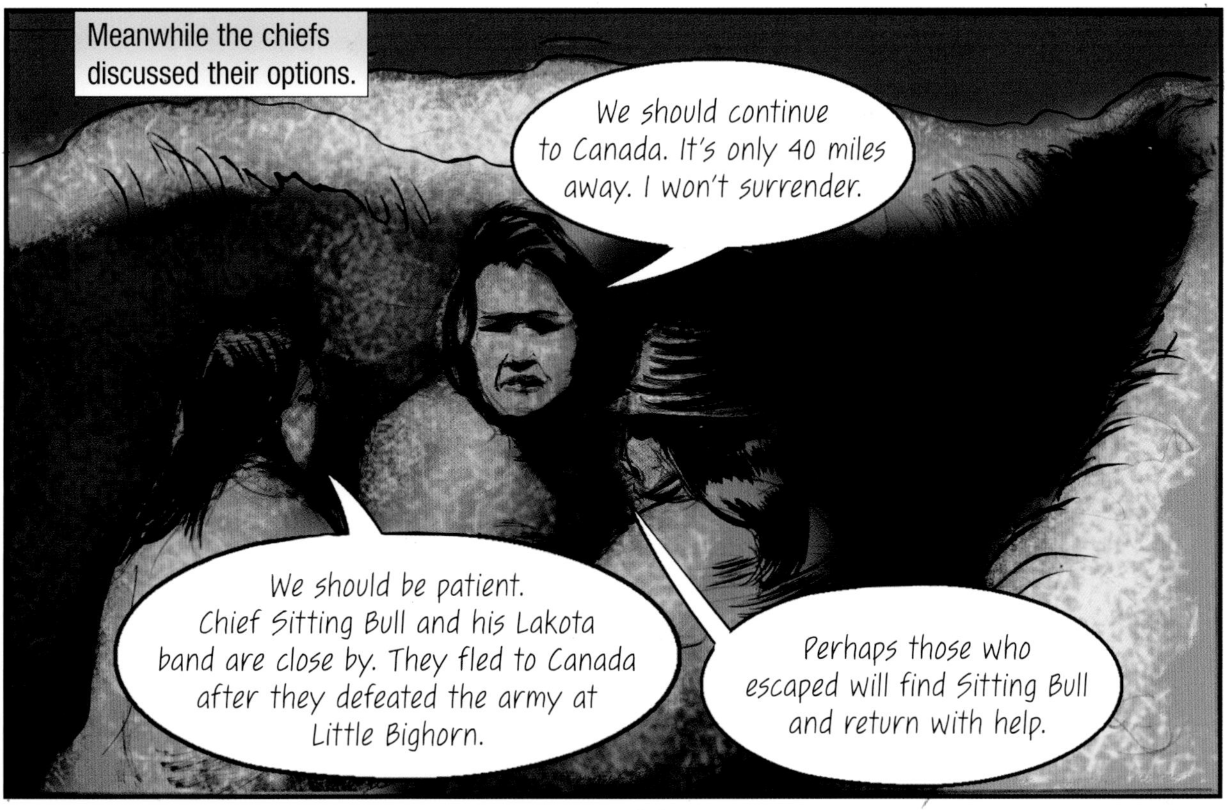

Meanwhile the chiefs discussed their options.
We should continue to Canada. It's only 40 miles away. I won't surrender.
We should be patient. Chief Sitting Bull and his Lakota band are close by. They fled to Canada after they defeated the army at Little Bighorn.
Perhaps those who escaped will find Sitting Bull and return with help.

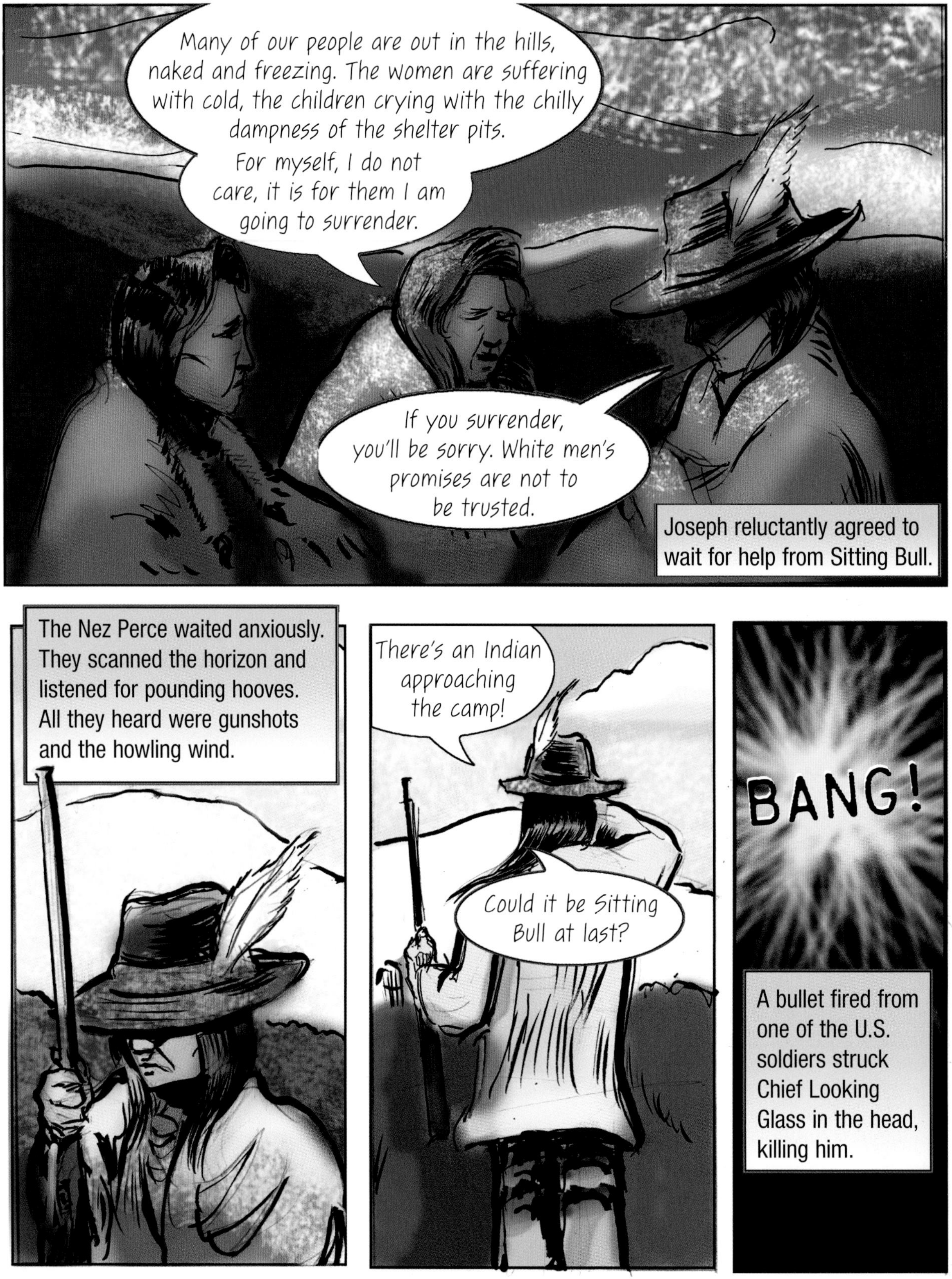

Many of our people are out in the hills, naked and freezing. The women are suffering with cold, the children crying with the chilly dampness of the shelter pits.
For myself, I do not care, it is for them I am going to surrender.
If you surrender, you'll be sorry. White men's promises are not to be trusted.
Joseph reluctantly agreed to wait for help from Sitting Bull.
The Nez Perce waited anxiously. They scanned the horizon and listened for pounding hooves. All they heard were gunshots and the howling wind.
There's an Indian approaching the camp!
Could it be Sitting Bull at last?
BANG!
A bullet fired from one of the U.S. soldiers struck Chief Looking Glass in the head, killing him.

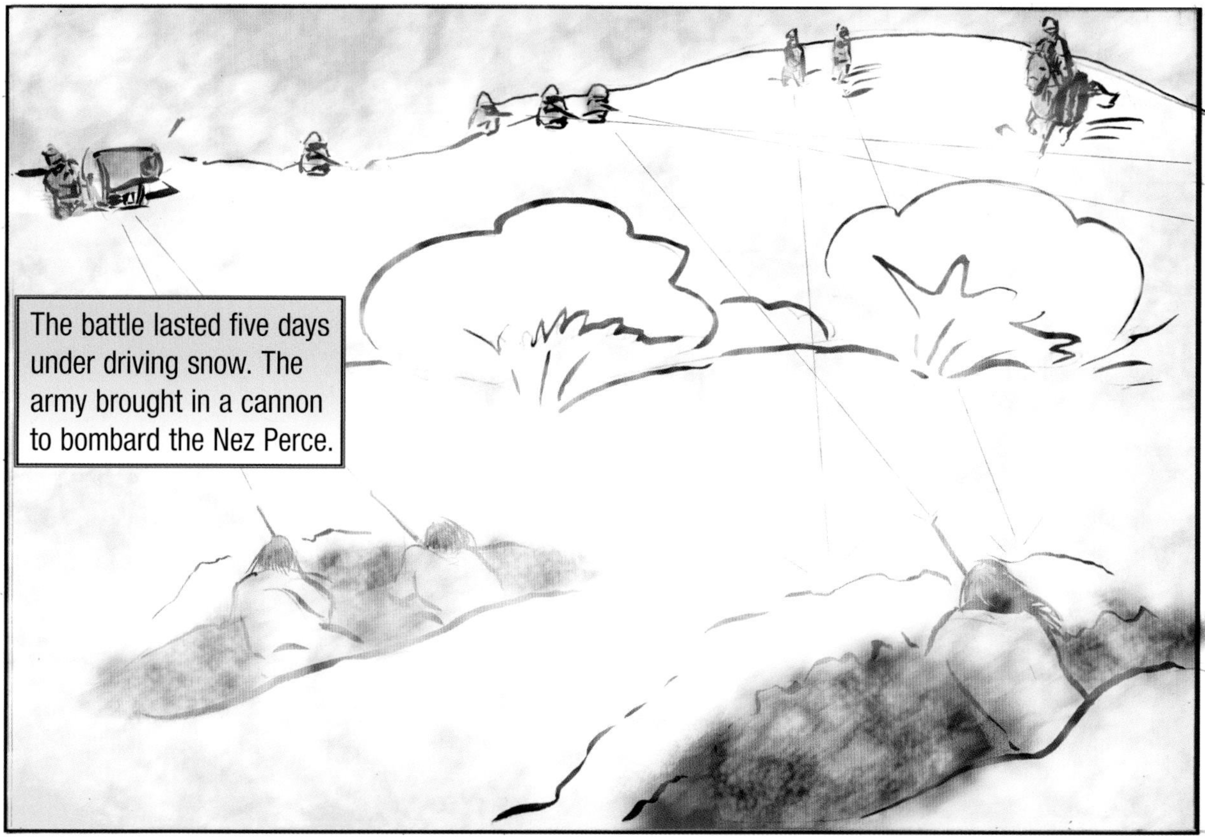
The battle lasted five days under driving snow. The army brought in a cannon to bombard the Nez Perce.

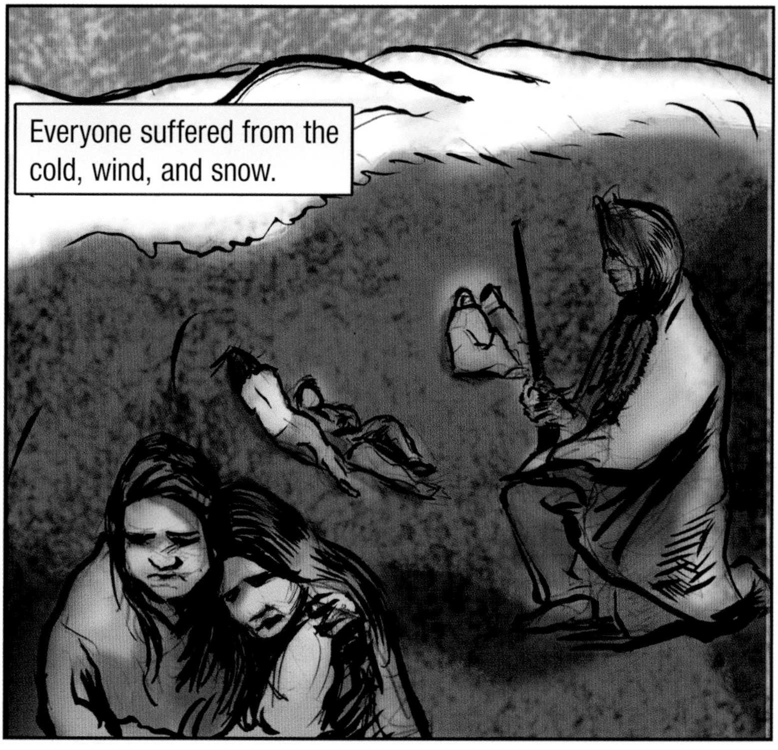
Everyone suffered from the cold, wind, and snow.

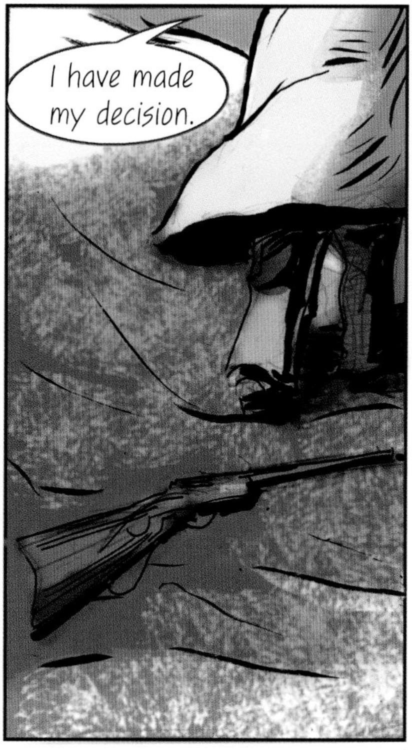
I have made my decision.

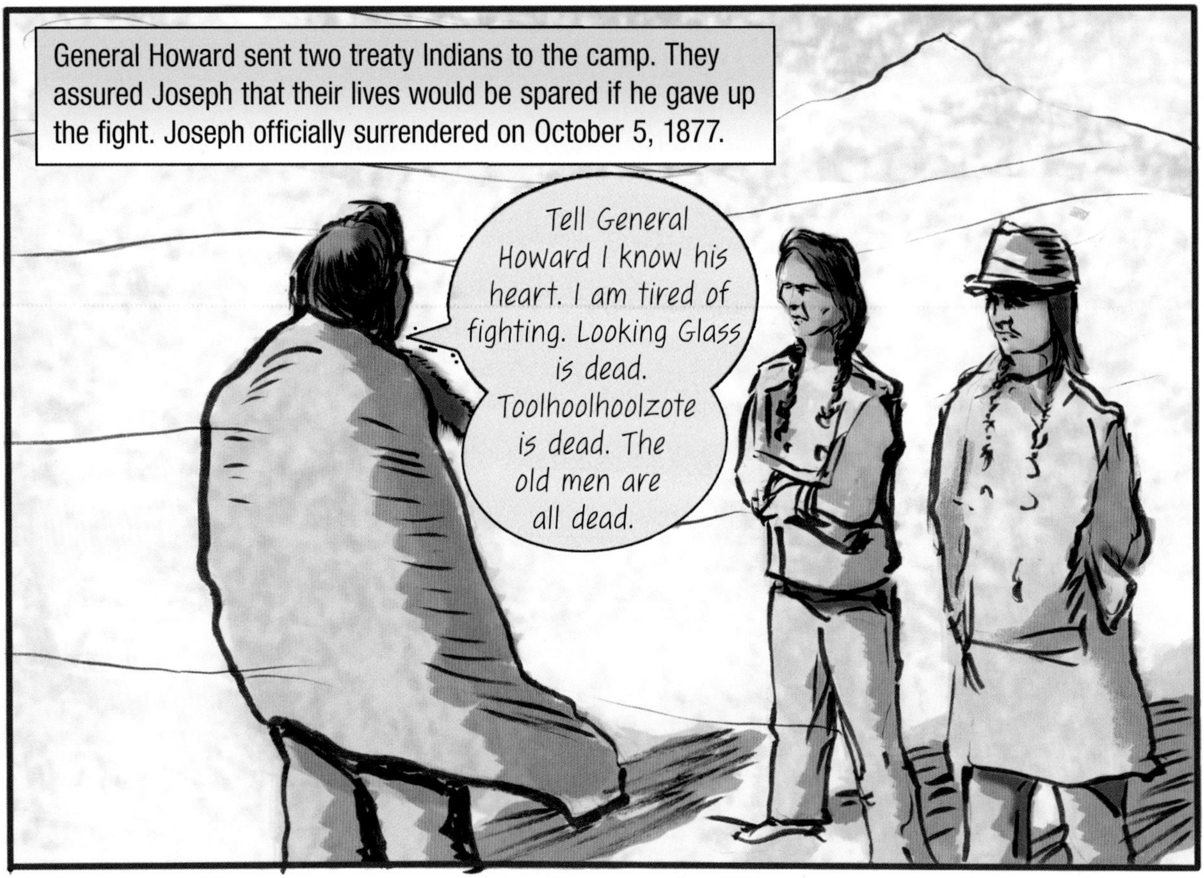
General Howard sent two treaty Indians to the camp. They assured Joseph that their lives would be spared if he gave up the fight. Joseph officially surrendered on October 5, 1877.
Tell General Howard I know his heart. I am tired of fighting. Looking Glass is dead. Toolhoolhoolzote is dead. The old men are all dead.

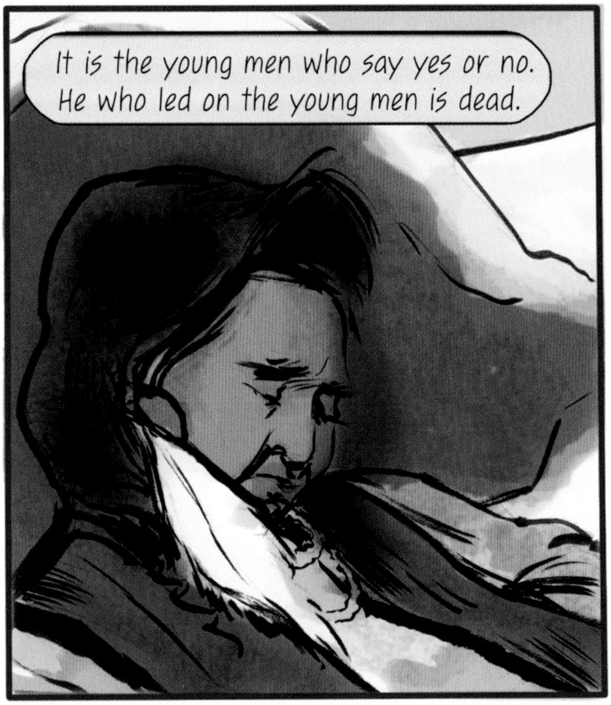
It is the young men who say yes or no. He who led on the young men is dead.

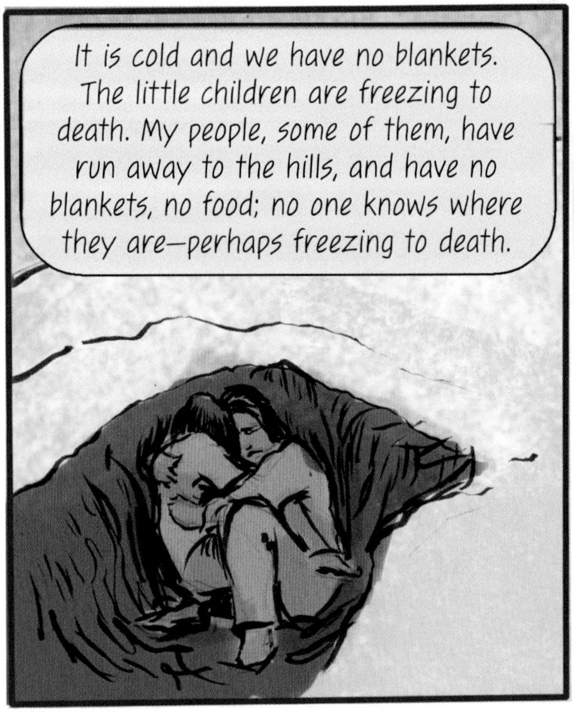
It is cold and we have no blankets. The little children are freezing to death. My people, some of them, have run away to the hills, and have no blankets, no food; no one knows where they are—perhaps freezing to death.

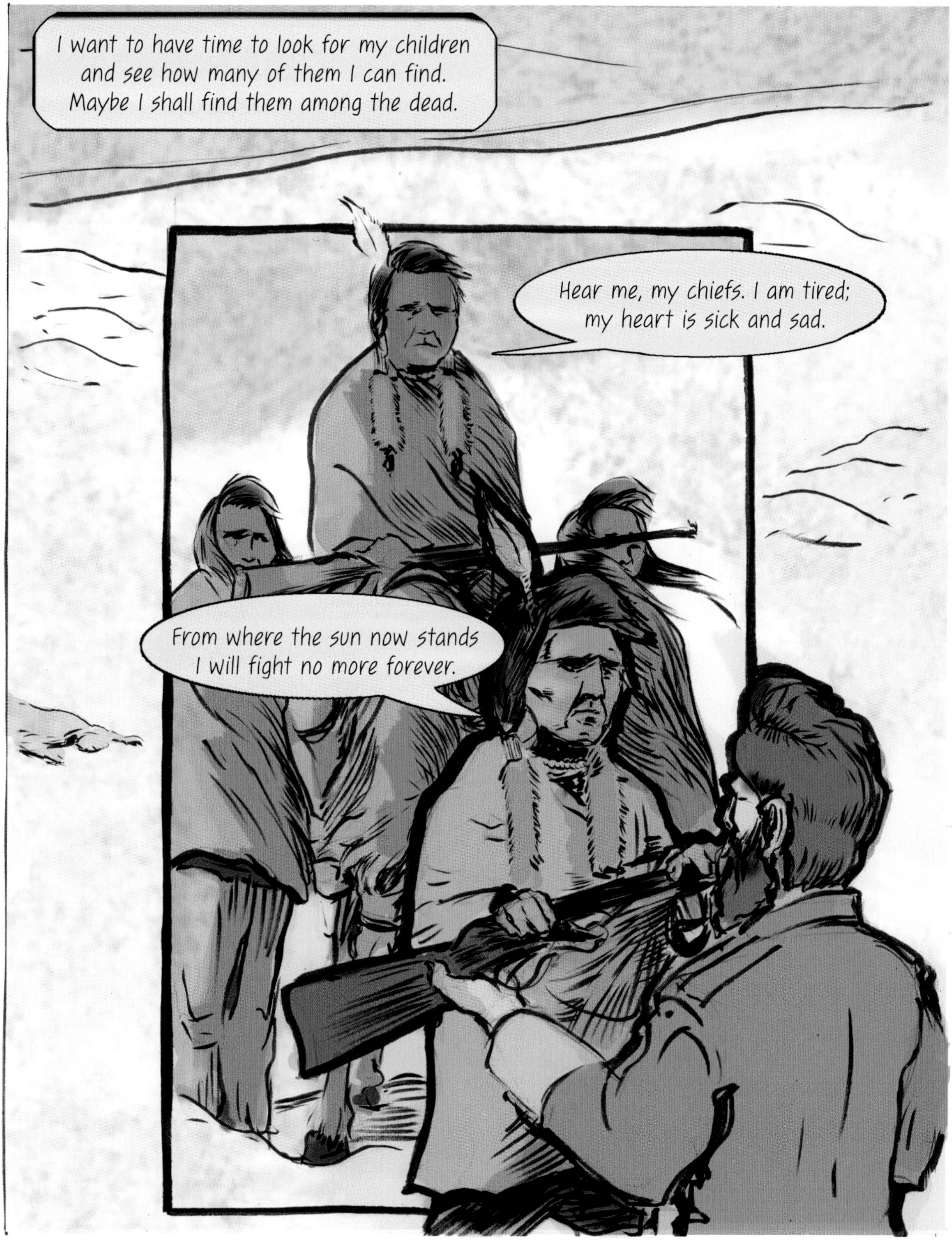

I want to have time to look for my children and see how many of them I can find. Maybe I shall find them among the dead.
Hear me, my chiefs. I am tired; my heart is sick and sad.
From where the sun now stands I will fight no more forever.

The earth is the mother of all people, and all people should have equal rights upon it.

~Chief Joseph

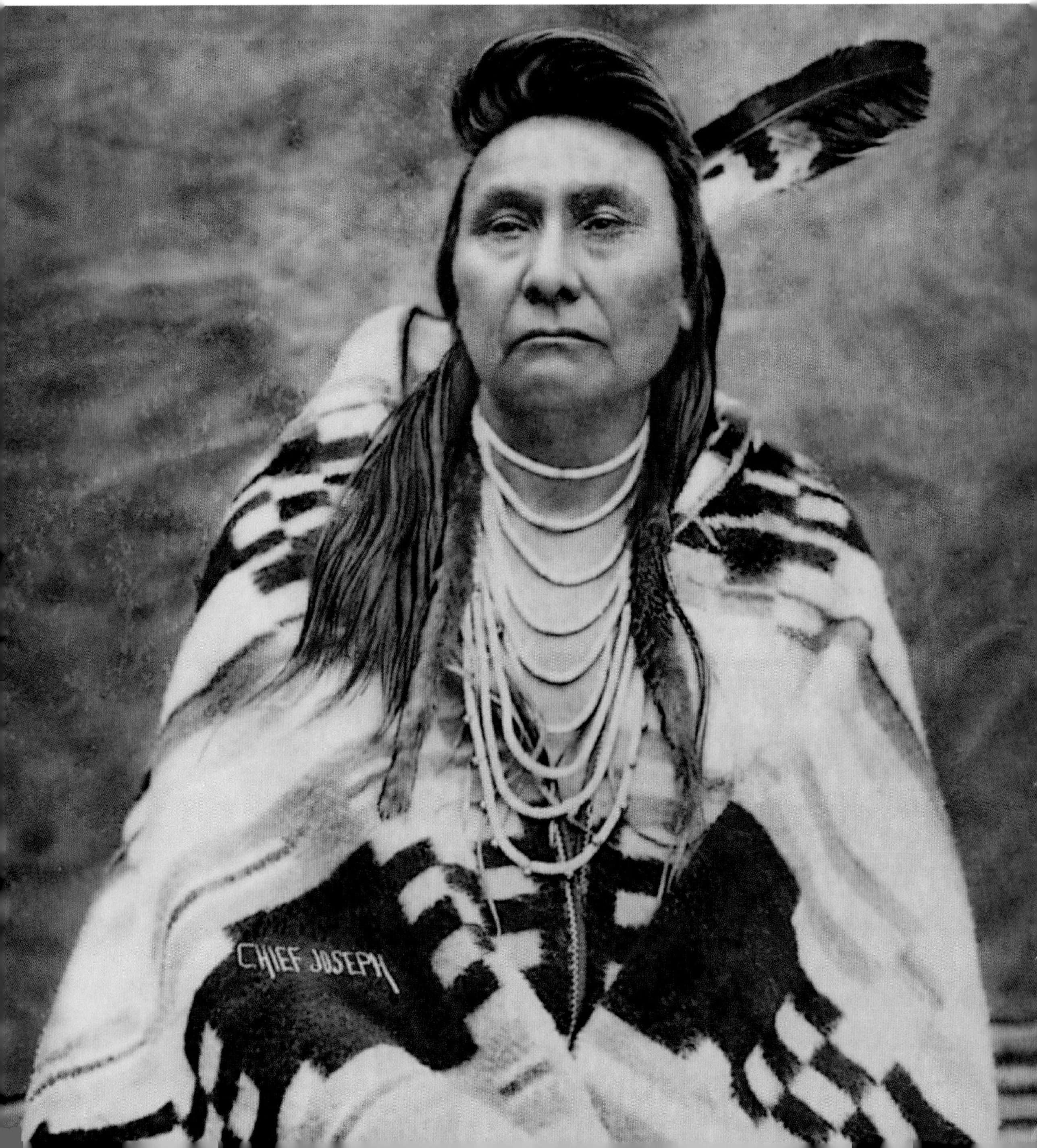
CHIEF JOSEPH

More About Chief Joseph

Joseph was born in 1840. His name, *Hin-mah-too-yah-lat-kekt*, means Thunder Rolling Down the Mountain. To whites, however, he was known as Joseph the Younger, or Chief Joseph. His father had taken the Christian name Joseph when he was baptized as an adult. Feeling betrayed by the treaties that took away his land, Old Joseph later gave up his Christian faith. He returned to the old ways of his ancestors, and raised his children in them as well.

After Joseph's surrender, Looking Glass' warning that the white man was not to be trusted turned out to be right. Instead of settling on the Lapwai reservation in Idaho as promised, Joseph and his people were sent to Oklahoma. Far from the cool mountains and valleys they knew, many Nez Perce died from heatstroke and disease.

Joseph never gave up fighting for his people. Instead of weapons, he used words. Thanks to the press accounts of the Nez Perce War and his surrender, Joseph was famous. He accepted every offer he had to speak and closed his speeches with visions of brotherhood: "We shall all be alike—brothers of one father and one mother, with one sky above us and one country around us and one government for all." Joseph soon became a spokesman not only for the Nez Perce, but also for the rights of all American Indians.

Joseph's speeches gained widespread sympathy for the Nez Perce cause. People from all over the country petitioned Congress to return the Nez Perce to their lands. Finally, in 1885, the 268 survivors were allowed to return to the Pacific Northwest. Joseph always hoped that one day he would return to his beloved Wallowa Valley, but federal authorities never allowed it. He died at Colville, Washington in 1904 at the age of 64.

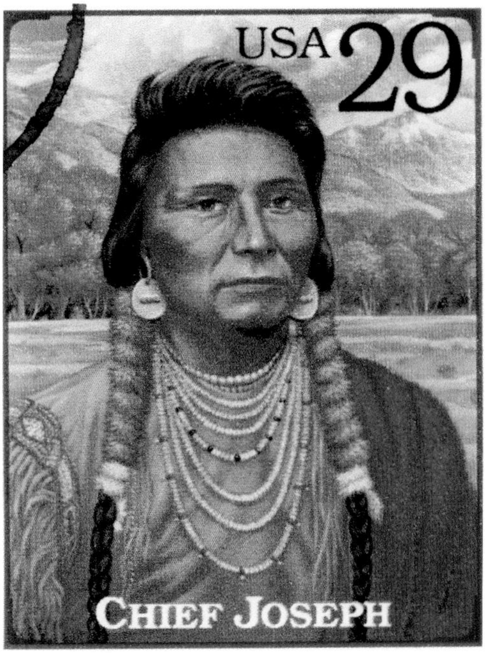
USA 29
CHIEF JOSEPH

1994 U.S. postage stamp

Glossary

appeal (uh-PEEL)—to ask for something urgently

bombard (bom-BAHRD)—to attack a place with heavy gunfire

cavalry (KA-vuhl-ree)—soldiers who travel and fight on horseback

negotiate (ni-GOH-shee-ate)—to discuss an issue with someone who does not hold the same view so that an agreement can be made

petition (puh-TISH-uhn)—to make a formal request to an authority with respect to a particular cause

reinforcements (ree-in-FORSS-muhnts)—extra troops sent into battle

reservation (rez-er-VAY-shuhn)—an area of land set aside by the U.S. government for American Indians

surrender (suh-REN-dur)—to give up or admit defeat in battle

territory (TER-uh-tor-ee)—the land and waters under control of a state, nation, or ruler

treaty (TREE-tee)—an official agreement between two or more groups or countries

trench (TRENCH)—a long, deep area cut into the ground with dirt piled up on one side

truce (TROOSS)—an agreement to stop fighting while peace is discussed

weary (WEER-ee)—very tired or exhausted

Read More

Dennis, Yvonne Wakim and Arlene Hirschfelder. *A Kid's Guide to Native American History: More than 50 Activities.* Chicago: Chicago Review Press, 2010.

Gunther, Vanessa. *Chief Joseph: A Biography.* Greenwood Biographies. Santa Barbara, Calif.: ABC-CLIO, 2010.

Hopping, Lorraine Jean. *Chief Joseph: The Voice for Peace.* Sterling Biographies. New York: Sterling, 2009.

Internet Sites

FactHound offers a safe, fun way to find Internet sites related to this book. All of the sites on FactHound have been researched by our staff.

Here's all you do: Visit *www.facthound.com*

Type in this code: 9781429654722

Super-cool stuff!

Check out projects, games and lots more at
www.capstonekids.com

Index

AMERICAN GRAPHIC